ALLEN RIDER GUIDES

RIDING TO HOUNDS

ALLEN RIDER GUIDES

Riding to Hounds

John Williams

J. A. Allen

London

British Library Cataloguing in Publication Data
Williams, John, 1929–
   Riding to hounds. – (Allen's rider guides)
   1. Great Britain. Hunting with hounds
   I. Title
   799.2'34

   ISBN 0–85131–463–5

Published in Great Britain in 1989 by
J A Allen & Company Limited
1, Lower Grosvenor Place
London SW1W 0EL

Printed in Great Britain by
WBC Print Ltd, Bristol

Contents

List of Illustrations

Introduction

So you want to go hunting. Indeed, as you have bought this book you probably want to go on a horse; and I expect you also want to know rather more about it than you do at this moment.

Hunting is a difficult subject about which to generalise. With over 300 hunts in the British Isles, whose followers ride horses, there is plenty of scope for variety. No two of about 200 packs of foxhounds are identical. Variation results from where the hunt is, the type of hounds it has, the kind of countryside it crosses, the personalities of the people principally involved, and, last but not least, the amount of money available for organisation. Finally, there is that other important local factor: tradition. Tradition can cause a multitude of differences from where the hunt meets and the days on which it does so, to what one wears and the type of hounds one follows.

Therefore before you wind a stock-tie carefully around your neck, thrust the pin through it, and into your jugular vein, pull on a pair of over-tight black riding boots and cram a hard protecting hat upon your head, it is as well to know something about the hunt you intend to go out with.

First, of course, you need to know the name of the hunt, where they intend to meet and at what time. Then you need to know if you may go out, and if so what financial contribution you will be required to make. Finally, if you do not wish to stand out unduly, it is probably as well to know the type of dress normally worn by most followers of that particular hunt.

If this information cannot be obtained from a friend who is a regular follower of the hunt, then the hunt secretary will normally be pleased to supply it. His or her name and address can be found in the appropriate hunting numbers of *Horse and*

Hound, or in the current volume of *Baily's Hunting Directory*. *Baily's* is published by J. A. Allen and contains details of most packs of hounds world-wide – it is helpful to have a copy available.

However, there is more to hunting than just knowing where to go, what to wear, and what to do. Therefore, this book includes discussions and explanations on what a hunt is, its organisation and its place in the countryside as a whole, the morality of hunting, what one hunts with – horses and hounds, and the hunted – foxes, deer and hares.

Nearly twenty years ago I wrote a small book called *An Introduction to Hunting*. Much of what I said then is still true, however, even the hunting world changes and it has therefore been decided to produce a new book; one that sits comfortably within the *Rider Guide* series.

The object of this small book is to help someone who is intending to start hunting, and to give him or her the basic information which will help them to do so, and with as little expense as possible. Once you have started there are a great many other books available, both fact and fiction, to increase your hunting knowledge; the more you know the more you are likely to want to know.

There are some words used in the text the meanings of which may be obscure, but the definitions can be found in the Glossary at the end.

1 The Morality of Hunting

Man is different from the other animals that inhabit this earth. It is a matter of belief that he has a soul, it is a matter of fact that there are two other major differences.

First, man is able to communicate with others of the same species in great detail. Second, animals are slaves of the environment that is created for them by God, by nature, or by man. Man, on the other hand, has the power to largely create his own environment.

The first of these differences has resulted in man's development from an omnivorous animal, hunting to live, to a creature specialising in an artificial way of life which sometimes gives him no natural contact with the plants and animals that maintain life.

The second has resulted in his being able to control not only animal numbers, but also their conditions of life. Indeed, he is largely responsible, both directly and indirectly, for the amount of life that can be supported. Such power brings with it privileges. It enables him to use animal life for his own benefit, and he can also breed and develop new types of animal for his own domestic use. It also allows him to protect from other animals that which he grows, but it brings with it both moral and practical responsibilities; responsibilities to the animals themselves and to the future generations that will succeed him.

He must, therefore, use his power so that control is carried out humanely and he must do it in such a way so as not to upset the essential balance of nature. If it is within his power to destroy he must use that power with great care lest the chain of destruction, once started, brings with it irreversible decline.

How is hunting affected by these responsibilities? First of all, if it is man's prerogative to use animal and hence wild life for his own advantage, then of course he may hunt, provided there is no infringement of his responsibility to preserve and prevent suffering. Let us consider the following.

To begin with it is obvious that the *organised* sport of hunting maintains a species in existence. If one plays tennis one does not start the game by throwing away all the balls, but if there are too many balls on the court one removes the surplus. Similarly, hunting aims to control the numbers of the hunted. A reasonable amount live; the old, the weak, the injured and otherwise superfluous die. The species survives; it remains strong and healthy. It is when hunting becomes disorganised that there is risk, for then there are no rules and no-one knows the state of play.

With regard to suffering, there are two kinds – physical and mental. Physical suffering in the wild is usually caused by injury or starvation. A wild animal has no vet or doctor to look after it if it is injured, therefore if its numbers are to be controlled humanely they must be reduced in a way which leaves no chance of the animal's escape in an injured condition, perhaps to linger until exhaustion or starvation brings death.

Of all the methods of control, hunting alone either kills the animal concerned or leaves it totally uninjured. It is a sophistication of the natural method, for most wild animals are killed by others under the never-ending principles of the survival of the fittest. However, because it is a sophistication, most forms of hunting take place only during the autumn and winter, a period when the young are no longer dependent on their mothers for food. Physical suffering also takes place when the mother of young, still unable to look after themselves, dies; death by starvation is their inevitable end, and it is ironic that in a supposedly civilised world it is only the ethics of hunters that give the hunted a chance to rear their young in safety! Hunting is a sport but it is also a balanced and humane way of control.

Mental suffering is far harder to estimate; but, it is a fact, that man has a much greater mental capacity than other animals. Both live by experience, but human experience is not only derived from what has happened to an individual, but also from what he has been told, read or seen. In short, human knowledge is the sum of human experience and an animal's knowledge is limited to its own experience.

In a hunted animal's experience, it has always been successful in a contest with hounds, otherwise it would not be alive. Indeed, it can be easily proved that most animals do not associate their own experience with that of other animals. A bunch of stags watching a hind being hunted in December will often take but a mild interest. In Africa antelope will continue to graze while a pride of lions devour one of their number at no great distance. Hunting may produce fear, but animals do not have the imagination that leaves man so petrified he may be unable to move.

Hunting guarantees that the animals it pursues do not suffer from injury, it guarantees a closed season for some of the hunted, and produces a means of control which supports the law of nature, enabling the fit and strong to survive while the weak and the old die in a world where there is no-one to look after them. This is all done at the price of an element of fear which is proveably not excessive.

However, even if hunting is humane, how does it fit into the social structure of Great Britain at the end of the twentieth century? In the last twenty years the countryside has altered out of all recognition. Many villages are now largely occupied by commuters, or those who have retired; other houses belong to week-enders or people with second homes. Agriculture has altered to an even greater extent. It has become so efficient that it produces more food than there is a market for, and in doing so it has altered the face of the land. Finally, television has created a degree of urban interest in rural subjects which – together with the immense development of the roads – has brought large numbers of city dwellers into the countryside for an increasing amount of their spare time. It is therefore hardly surprising that they are concerned about what they see, nor is it surprising that they frequently get very involved with these concerns.

In 1988 'conservation' is a big word. How does hunting fit in with the conservation of the countryside? First of all it must be realised what one is trying to conserve. Conservation is concerned with species not with individuals. Thus if an oak wood is felled, conservation demands that another is planted in its place; it does not demand that all oaks are left standing until they fall down due to disease, old age, or accident. Conservation of the countryside concerns the provision of habitat, and the supply of food and water for wild animals and birds. It is not concerned with the death of a fox, it is concerned with the fox population and the position of foxes in the balance of nature.

For generations hunting has been concerned with conservation. The countryside that we are now trying so hard to conserve was largely created by the combined efforts of farmers and their landlords. Indeed, while the former divided up the fields with walls or hedges to contain their stock, landowners planted and retained small coverts for the benefit of game. Even as recently as 1985, a survey showed that over 80 per cent of the small woodlands planted in the previous decade were put there with either hunting or shooting as the principal reason for their existence.

Whatever the reason for the woodlands being planted, they provide an invaluable habitat for many different kinds of bird, animal and plant. If managed with birds or animals in mind, they are usually left quiet during the breeding season, a fact appreciated by all forms of wild life. Size and type are also of primary importance. Twenty 10 acre blocks of such woodland provide far more habitat for wildlife than a single block of 200 acres. The reasons for this are: firstly there is less actual competition for territories if there is more space; animals, like people, prefer to live with the neighbours not too close, and secondly, twenty 10 acre blocks have arithmetically several times as much edge or perimeter as one 200 acre block. It is cover near to the outside edge where there is both light and shade that is of greatest value to most forms of flora and fauna.

It is also important to a healthy breeding population that families should be split up; mating then takes place outside rather than inside the family circle. Once again, this is more likely where coverts are numerous and not too large.

In fact, this natural balance has been maintained for more than 100 years by field sports interests, though recent farming developments have sometimes put it under strain. However, although the removal of fences and the drainage of bogs have been a disadvantage both to hunting and animals, most small coverts still remain and so do many fences. Hunting and the love of sport have helped both to survive and there is no doubt that they will continue to do so.

Hunting is, therefore, humane, and it is a major force for conservation, but how does it affect other people's lives? There is no doubt that it occasionally creates problems. Hounds are trained to hunt an animal, and use their noses to follow its scent. Sometimes the hunt staff are not able to get to them and on these occasions they may not be able to stop the hounds even if it would be advisable. On other occasions hunt followers can cause congestion on the roads and it is true that those same followers can cause damage and leave gates open that should be shut. Why then do most farmers welcome the hounds?

It is partly tradition and partly the fact that the killing and movement of red deer and foxes is helpful. But it is also due to the social value of the hunt within the community. Not only does a hunt provide sport for its followers, but both it and its Supporters Club create a social base for a large part of the rural community. It is a base that covers a cross section of people. Such social events as the point-to-point and the hunt ball are due to it, but so too are numerous other events such as village hops and darts or skittle matches. Lord Willoughby de Broke once described hunting as 'the golden thread that binds the countryside together'; that is still true, for hunting is a link that binds men and women of many kinds and all social classes. It is a link which is invaluable in an age when there appear to be so many things to divide us and so few to join us.

2 What is a Hunt?

In 1986 the various hunting associations recognised 446 packs of hounds within the British Isles. Of these, 144 were followed on foot, while in 302 the horse as well as the hound played a prominent part.

A few of those packs were privately owned. Two were the property of limited companies and the remainder belonged to the Hunt Committees which controlled them. Indeed, in the matter of organisation there is a surprising similarity between hunting and Association Football. There is after all nothing to prevent a man kicking a ball about, but for his team to become part of the football league it has to be recognised by the Football Association and obey its rules. Similarly, there is nothing to stop a man taking a few hounds out on land where he has permission to go. However, for him to be recognised by one of the Hunting Associations, he has to have an agreed area or 'country' where he has permission to go, and he has to agree to be bound by the rules of that relevant association.

Indeed, the resemblance goes much further. Football Clubs are controlled by a Chairman and a board of directors who hand over the day to day organisation to a Manager. Most hunts are controlled by a Chairman and Committee who hand over the day to day control to a Master or joint Masters, people whom they appoint on an annual basis.

Both Masters and Manager are responsible for the standard of sport they provide and both have to do this within the financial restrictions placed upon them. They are also responsible for the work force at their disposal. In the one case, players, in the other, hounds and hunt staff. In both cases too there is a considerable back-up force of people who, though vitally important, are often largely unseen; they may be professionals, part-time workers, or dedicated amateurs.

Finally, within the Football League there are a few very rich clubs based on the major centres of population. They have many of the best players, probably the best grounds, and they receive much of what desirable publicity there is. In the countryside some hunts work on far larger budgets than others. They have good country to ride over but in this they are not unique. The fact is that they are usually within easy range of large numbers of people; with the result that they have the financial strength to make full use of the land that they do have. Hunts such as the Quorn and the Duke of Beaufort's are no more typical of most hunts than Liverpool or Manchester United are typical of most football clubs, but they set a standard which is respected and sometimes envied.

If you look at the 302 hunts in which horses are involved, you will find that six have packs of hounds hunting deer. There are fifty packs of harriers hunting either hares or foxes, and ten packs who follow a drag-line. Five packs of bloodhounds follow the 'clean boot', or in other words hunt men, and the remaining 231, more than three-quarters of the hunts involved, hunt and catch foxes.

Therefore, before we go hunting we need to see how they work and understand who does what and where. It is of course true that in some of the smaller hunts a great many corners are cut. Masters work extremely hard and may rely upon enthusiastic but unskilled labour. Even in the largest ones some economies are made. However, where funds are available the labour force is usually as described.

It divides into three groups: those who work with the hounds, with the horses, and in the countryside. All three groups are under the orders of the Master.

The Master

The Master, or Masters, are in daily control of the hunt. They employ the hunt servants and they arrange the meets. In most cases they will themselves do a great deal of work in the countryside. They will see the farmers over whose land they expect to go, and perhaps some of those where they have been.

They will arrange the earth-stopping and will do their best to ensure that the country is crossable on a horse. They will also make certain that the huntsman and Field Master (and they themselves are likely to be one or the other) know the exact position of any particular piece of land where they may not go. They should also know more general problems of terrain that they are likely to meet. In doing this, they will be helped by their hunt secretary, and they may well have a full time fencer, but they are more likely to have the help of voluntary labour or part-time employees. Tradition and habit may dictate how the work is done – what matters is that it *is* done.

The Kennels

HUNTSMAN AND KENNEL-HUNTSMAN In charge of the kennels will be the huntsman or – if the Master hunts the hounds himself – the kennel-huntsman. It is his responsibility to look after the hounds. He takes care of them in the kennels and (if huntsman) controls them when they are out hunting. He exercises them, looks after their health, feeds them and cares for their puppies. He manages them by using his voice, and, when out hunting, his horn. For them, he is the leader of their pack and he receives their respect and affection. For him, they are his children of whom he is fond but with whom he is firm.

WHIPPERS-IN A hunt has one or two whippers-in to assist the huntsman. In the kennel they help him look after the hounds, and take their orders from him in the hunting field. The huntsman will expect them to be alert and keep an eye on the proceedings, to help him collect hounds that have been left behind, or stop those that are hunting the wrong quarry. If the whippers-in are in the wrong place at the wrong time, the huntsman is to blame.

THE KENNELMAN This man also receives his orders from the huntsman. He has the important job of collecting and preparing the food for the hounds. To do this he will take the hunt's 'knacker-van' on a round of farms collecting animals that have died, these he then skins and cuts up. In some kennels the food is cooked, but in most it is fed raw. In addition, it is the kennelman's job to see that the kennels are kept clean and the bedding changed when necessary.

The Stables

THE STUD-GROOM   In charge of the stables, is a stud-groom, and he will have under him a number of under-grooms. The number he has depends upon the number of horses, and that depends on the number of people he has to mount and the number of days per week he has to do it. There can of course be no fixed rule, but an average figure may be a total of one or two more than one per man per day in the week hunted, for the hunt stables usually have the odd casualty.

OTHER OFFICIALS   Finally, there are other officials, for most hunts are at the centre of a large number of activities that take place in the countryside. Some of these activities are run by the hunts' Supporters Clubs, others – such as the point-to-points and hunter trials, have organising bodies of their own. All of them require chairmen, secretaries etc., and they too are a part of a hunt's organisation.

3 The Different Types of Hunting

Why People Hunt

There are three main reasons why people go hunting. Some enjoy seeing hounds work; they are enthralled by the contest between a pack of hounds with their huntsman and an animal renowned throughout history for its cleverness. Then there are those whose main enjoyment is the ride; people who find infinite pleasure in riding a horse over unknown country and an unprepared line of obstacles; people who find that the excitement of the chase sets their adrenalin going and their blood pumping. Finally, there are those who enjoy the social side and find the atmosphere convivial, people who both find and make friends in the hunting field and its connected events. In fact, most people enjoy all three aspects and it is the balance of importance between them that varies from person to person. Indeed, it is this balance – together with where you live and what you can afford – that will probably decide where you hunt.

I have said that in 1986 there were 302 hunts whose hounds were followed by a mounted field. They had six different kinds of quarry, but the majority hunted foxes. Fifty were packs of harriers who traditionally hunt hares. In the counties of Devon and Somerset three packs pursued wild red deer. In the New Forest, a solitary pack of hounds hunted the fallow buck. In Ireland two packs followed the carted deer. The final fifteen packs all followed men: ten had a drag line laid by a man and the other five were packs of bloodhounds who hunted man himself.

With different quarries and different types of hounds, it is hardly surprising that what is likely to happen also differs.

Foxhunting

One of the things that appeals to many people about foxhunting is the degree to which it is totally unpredictable. A good day depends upon so many things. Some of them are known: the country that one is to hunt over, the ability of the hounds and their huntsman, and the general efficiency of the organisation. They are the reasons which bring a large number of followers to a popular meet in a fashionable country. On their own however, they do not guarantee a good day for that depends even more on other factors such as the existing weather and through it the scenting conditions that exist. Then there is the behaviour and mentality of the individual foxes that are found. Thus, if you hunt one fox for forty minutes on a reasonable scent you may finish within a few yards of where it was found, having never left the parish, while with another, you may be several miles away after going straight across country from one district to another.

One of the great things about the British Isles is the variety that exists within a comparatively limited area: variety of topography, variety of soil and underlying rock, variety of people. It has been my great good fortune to hunt with nearly 100 packs of hounds, yet no two were the same. Woodland and moorland, plough and grass, hedge, fence, ditch and bank, all differ and provide different stages on which hunting takes place, but it is the people – and particularly the local people – who give it its character and provide its strength.

The fox

Hare Hunting

Harriers, like foxhounds, hope to have two or three different hunts during each day. Traditionally, they are easier-going than foxhounds. Hares tend to run in circles or at least confine their activities to comparatively limited areas. As a result, there is seldom the rush and hurry that foxhunting produces.

In addition, it is usually easier to see what the hounds are doing. For most hares are found by hounds drawing in the open, or are put up by members of the Field as they cross the country. Hares turn, twist, run their own line and eventually lie down; foxes usually keep going. The result is that the harrier huntsman must be patient, while with foxhounds time is of the essence. Similarly, the harrier huntsman will often cast back while with foxhounds the tendency is to go forward.

The hare

All in all, if you have a pack of harriers hunting hares in your locality, you may well learn a great deal about hunting if you go out with them; but they will not often generate the sustained excitement and urgency of a good pack of foxhounds.

Red Deer Hunting

Staghunting, as it is carried out in Devon and Somerset, is in some ways the purest form of hunting because hounds go out with the intention of hunting one particular deer. It is an animal which has been harboured or located during the previous night or in the early morning of the day concerned.

It is roused by a few hounds known as tufters, and it is

separated from any other deer in the locality by them. Once this has been achieved, it is given a start while the main body of the pack are sent for. They are then laid on the line and the hunt gets underway. From that moment on, the whole day's sport depends on the ability of the hounds to keep to that one animal, while the deer – by nature a herd animal – will try to join up with other deer. The hunt may last from one or two hours to six or seven, but there is one quarry and one quarry only.

Tufting usually takes place in woodland where a large number of horses would be a considerable hindrance and so this vital part of the day is left to the hunt staff and a few of the most knowledgeable followers. On occasions however, particularly when the deer are on the open moor, the Field may be allowed to follow and witness the selection of the harboured stag.

The red deer

However, never forget the need to conserve your horse's energy. Staghunting, like hare hunting, does not have the urgency of foxhunting. The scent lasts longer and if you are in too much of a hurry your horse is likely to be tired well before the deer.

Hind hunting is similar to staghunting, but it is usually the herd rather than the individual that is harboured and tufting is not always carried out. However, because there are more hinds than stags and because they are less easily recognised, it is harder to prevent the hounds getting on to fresh deer.

With both stags and hinds, a successful hunt is concluded when the deer turns to face the hounds who will then bay at it. The huntsman carries a humane killer and a hunt official carries a gun on his saddle. The deer is then shot from close range where there is no chance of it being injured.

Buckhunting in the New Forest

In the New Forest, it is only the bucks who are hunted, never the does. Harbouring takes place as with the red deer, but because deer are also killed with a rifle, hunting does not have to carry out the degree of control that it does in the West Country. However, it is also true that the New Forest buckhounds are sometimes used to find and despatch deer which are known to be injured from road accidents or poaching (the hunt staff using humane killers). Hounds are also used on occasion, particularly in the spring, to move deer back into the Forest from private grazing around the Forest perimeter.

Carted Stag Hunting

The two packs of staghounds that hunt the carted deer both exist in Ireland. Before the last war there were a number of such packs in England, but most of them never restarted and those that did ceased to exist in the early fifties.

As a sport, it provides an exciting ride across country. The hunt starts when a deer is released from a cart or waggon, and ends when it turns at bay. The deer is then reloaded into its transport and returned home. Many of the deer used are well known characters and have considerable personal reputations with their followers, indeed the fact that a specific animal is to be used on a particular day may well be responsible for the numbers of people at the meet.

Draghunting

Most packs of drag hounds provide a fast, exhilarating ride in a limited period of time. Meets often take place in the afternoon; the hounds follow an artificial lure, which is usually woollen material sewn into a sausage and soaked in a chemical liquid giving off a pungent scent. Because it is dragged or pulled by a runner, it can also be lifted, thus producing a check. This makes it possible for drag hounds to have a series of short bursts. They

Hounds follow an artificial lure

are therefore able to provide fun where both time and space are limited. However, it does not produce the uncertainty and excitement of hunting a wild animal, for someone always knows the line that is due to be taken, and often most people do, as the majority of drag hunts have specific lines which follow certain meets – you gallop and jump, but there is no uncertainty about the start and no object at the end.

Hunting the 'Clean Boot'

There are two major differences between draghunting and hunting the 'clean boot'.

First, the animal doing the hunting is the slower-paced bloodhound rather than an ex-foxhound. It does not therefore have the drive and urgency of the latter, so the speed is not as great.

Secondly, of even more importance, is the fact that it is the man himself who is being hunted, not something that can be picked up or put down. The quarry is given a half-hour start to cover a leg of approximately six miles wearing leather boots which will leave a scent. Scent will also be picked up from hands and clothing brushing against gates, fences and undergrowth. The quarry may run two or three legs if very fit, but often two people will be used during the day and hounds will be shown an article of clothing belonging to the runner at the start of the line. As the bloodhound is an accomplished tracker, the scent is rarely lost and the hunt is usually steady and predictable.

Choosing the Type of Hunt

Having chosen a hunt from the alternatives that exist, you must ensure that which you choose is possible. The Master or hunt secretary will tell you whether or not you may go out, and will inform you of the rules that apply to that particular hunt. While all packs welcome their own members and farmers, there is sometimes a waiting list for new subscribers, and there is usually a limit on the numbers who wish to have an odd day's hunting.

4 The Horse

Riding to Hounds is the title of this book, and indeed for some people that is what hunting is all about – riding. Even among those whose principal object it is to ride rather than to hunt, the actual requirements differ. Some count every fence, and their hunting diaries largely contain what they and their horses jumped. Others are content with the sheer pleasure of riding with friends in beautiful country along with the excitement of the day; while yet others have the very special pleasure of bringing on and developing a young horse. All are welcome, for hunting is not and should not be made into a competitive sport. Indeed, though arriving close to hounds at the end of a fast hunt sends many a person home with a mental glow, others, who enjoy the intricate pleasures of a nice steady hunt, find the pressures of a fast hunt all too much.

The Right Horse

The most important requirement if you are going to enjoy your hunting is to have the right horse. How good an animal it has to be depends upon what you want it to do, and the country in which you are going to hunt. Of course it must be strong enough to carry your weight over the type of country your hunt usually crosses. Thus if the pack you intend to follow spends most of its time on heavy clay you will require a stronger, tougher horse to carry you than if it is chalk downland.

Similarly, if most fences are big thorn ones with a ditch, one needs a horse with the ability to spread itself; a very different animal altogether from what may be required in a small trappy country where drops, posts-and-rails or walls provide the standard fare. Some people are put off hunting after a short time by having horses that do not suit either them or the country they are in. What you need is an animal that suits you. General appearance and weight carrying ability are important in a hunter, but I believe the premier requirements are: fitness (as opposed to freshness), soundness, good manners, and an ability to jump willingly the sort of fences that you are likely to meet.

If you are starting to hunt and already have your own horse then the animal does, presumably, suit you already, but if you need to buy one you would be well advised to find the name of a reputable dealer, one who has supplied other people in the same hunt. Be honest with him, tell him how experienced you are and how much you are prepared to pay. Do not forget that most dealers who are recommended will have made their reputations by matching people with horses. If, as a result, you get what you want at a price you can afford, do not begrudge the dealer the money that he makes in doing a tricky job well. After all, you do not begrudge the tailor his profit if he makes your clothes fit!

If you are hiring a horse do not be tempted to over-estimate your riding ability and do try to ride the horse in advance to see if it suits you. It is absolutely essential for your own safety and that of others to remain in control. Always be guided by the owner of the horse or the proprietor of the riding establishment. Remember that a horse who is perfectly quiet and well-mannered on a familiar hack, may be almost uncontrollable by a novice in the excitement of the hunting field.

The Fitness and Care of the Hunter

Some of those who hunt to ride come to the Opening Meets at the start of November having had few, if any, days cubhunting. This may be deliberate, but it is more often a case of not being bothered or not having the time. The result may well be that neither they nor their horses are hunting fit. If the rider is not fit he will be sore at the end of the day, but if the horse is not fit it may well be injured or have an unnecessary fall. Pulled tendons and strained muscles in a horse are serious for they can easily make its first day in the hunting field its last.

Fresh horses too – ones that have too many oats and too little exercise – apart from being irritating mounts, can cause problems for other people by boiling over at all the wrong times.

Horses, like people, need a holiday. April, May and June are the best times for a hunter, for not only has the season just ended but the grass is also at its best. However, when the holiday is over, if the horse has been really let down, it needs bringing back up to fitness gently by plenty of steady exercise and a gradually increasing amount of protein, whether provided by oats or nuts. Good quality hay, and straw for bedding are important, for dust and mould can cause respiratory problems which affect condition.

If getting a horse fit is important, so too is getting it and its rider psychologically in tune. There is no doubt that this is done by the gradual build up of cubhunting from the first early mornings, to the enjoyable October days where much of the fun exists but the pressure and urgency are usually missing.

The care of the hunter, both before and after hunting is also extremely important. Other books in this series, *Riding Cross-Country* and *Riding Over Jumps*, deal with horse care pertinent to these two sports but hunting differs because the horse is ridden for far longer and the unpredictability of the day's sport is far greater. This can create problems in the stables. It means that the horse needs a good feed early in the morning, well before it is necessary to start getting it ready. It also means late nights as a horse's legs must be checked for cuts and thorns as they are cleaned off, before or after it has a hot feed.

The rider can save himself or others a great deal of work if he has brought his horse back to the horsebox gently – walking the last two miles or so rather than returning at a brisk trot. Walking will cool the horse and calm it. Once in the horsebox, the horse should have the saddle removed, a sweat rug, with a top-rug folded back from the shoulder, put on and have a hay-net to pick at. The horse then comes back to its stable in a relaxed frame of mind. There are few things more irritating than a strung-up animal refusing to eat its food and breaking out in a sweat time and again, besides which such an animal will not be able to go hunting again as quickly as one who has settled down.

If the horse is not yours or you do not have to look after it good manners dictate that you treat it as though it were your own – besides which it will probably pay in the long run, for you will be welcome rather than unwelcome on a second visit.

There are two other essentials if you are not to run the risk of spoiling what you expect to be a very enjoyable day:

TACK You require a saddle that fits both you and your horse and it needs to have been kept in good condition. If it does not fit the horse, or the girths are allowed to get loose, then the animal will probably get a sore back through friction and thus be put out of action. If the saddle does not fit you, or its surface is hard and dry, you will get a sore bottom! Then there is the question of the bit. You require a bit in the horse's mouth which suits it and which you can manage. Basically, you need the mildest one which gives you control, otherwise you may end up jumping on to someone who has fallen, or having to stop your horse by cannoning into someone else! Rubber-covered or laced reins assist grip as smooth wet reins slip through the fingers.

SHOEING There are few things as annoying as having to stop soon after the meet because your horse has lost a shoe. A good farrier is required, and shoes need checking both before and after hunting as does the state of the hoof. Many a hunter is put out of action by corns, or a cut caused by a shoe expected to do one day too many.

In conclusion, if you have a horse that is sound, fit and suits you, if it is well shod and its saddlery fits; if you have nice country and a good pack of hounds; if there is a scent and you find the right fox – then you may have a day you will remember for the rest of your life.

5 Hounds

To have a chapter about hounds themselves in a book that is about the riding side of hunting, may seem surprising. However, I believe that most people will enjoy themselves more if they know something about the background of the animals they follow.

Many of us look forward to a quick burst behind a flying pack, but such bursts are all too rare. In fact, much of most days' hunting will be spent standing still or moving comparatively slowly. If that time can be spent happily watching, then the pleasure gained from the day is increased. I believe that the more one knows, the more one enjoys oneself, and it is for this reason that I have written this chapter about the hounds themselves.

Hound Registration

The various hunting associations, and specifically the Masters of Foxhounds Association, are not like the Kennel Club in their treatment of both the hounds and their stud book. The Club is solely concerned with the pedigree of the animals it registers. The hunting associations are concerned not only with their pedigree but also with the use made of the hounds in their lifetime, and by whom it has been made.

Thus in the Masters of Foxhounds Association Rules it states that: '. . . To be eligible in the Foxhound Kennel Stud Book hounds must have been bred, "entered" and worked in a "recognised" Foxhound Kennel, besides which their sires and dams must have been "entered" and worked in a "recognised" Foxhound Kennel and registered in the Foxhound Kennel Stud Book'.

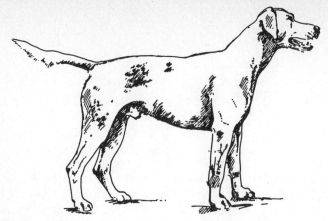

English foxhound

It then explains a complicated up-grading system in which the requirement is for five generations of known pedigree in which every hound has been kept to hunt foxes only in a recognised pack.

Harriers have a similar system, though in their case it is easier for hounds to be up-graded. However, in both cases the result is the same, namely that most kennels contain a cross created from different kinds of hound whose sole common denominator is that they and their ancestors have been kept to hunt one kind of animal.

Hounds Used for Foxhunting

There are seven different kinds of hound which are kept to hunt foxes alone in the British Isles, they are:
1) The American hound
2) The Dumfriesshire hound
3) The English foxhound
4) The Fell hound
5) The Kerry beagle
6) The Welsh hound
7) The West Country harrier

Of these, the American hound is limited to a few individuals. The Dumfriesshire are a carefully bred single pack of Anglo-

Welsh foxhound

French cross-breds, developed over a period of more than sixty years. The Kerry beagles are best known as the Black and Tans of Scarteen, but they have numerous connections with some other packs in Southern Ireland. The West Country harrier has all but died out in the pure state; but it still provides the dominant bloodlines for a number of West country packs which – though calling themselves harriers – have hunted foxes exclusively for a number of years.

There remains the English hound, the Welsh hound, and the Fell hound. Occasionally they are still found in the pure state, but when crossed they form the basis of most packs of foxhounds. Indeed, the life's work of some distinguished Masters has been the careful development of the crosses and lines which, in their opinion, suited both them and the countries they hunted.

Foxhunting as a sport takes place throughout the British Isles. It therefore takes place in areas that differ greatly. The variety stretches from the bleak mountains of Cumbria and Wales to the flat ploughs of East Anglia. It is a countryside which includes rolling hills based on chalk, granite or limestone as well as the clay- and silt-based river valleys, some of which form the grass vales of many of the most popular hunting countries.

Beagle

Change, however, concerns more than topography. It also concerns people. Hunting, and the love of hunting, seems to be universal among most genuine countrymen; but how they hunt varies with race and psychological make-up as well as with the land over which they hunt. It would therefore have been amazing had the types of hound, originally developed in the different regions to suit both the area and the people, not varied considerably.

Hound Qualities

The basic qualities that are required in a hound are the same everywhere. It is the balance in which they are held that varies. These qualities are:

1) *Nose* or scenting power so that the hound may follow the line left by its quarry, and to this must be added *perseverance* so that it will continue trying to use that scenting power even when the line is temporarily lost.

2) *Stamina* so that the hound can not only hunt one fox in each day, but, when required, several – and can keep on doing it on two or three days in each week throughout the winter.

3) *Tongue* or cry, so that not only is it able to smell a fox and hunt its line but that it lets others, both canine and human, know that it does.

4) *Pack sense* so that it works with other hounds and not as an

34

Bloodhound

individual, a quality closely linked to tongue for it is the individualist who is mute.

5) *Speed* so that the hound is able to put pressure on the fox when its scenting ability enables it to get near it. The hound also needs speed to keep in front of fast galloping horses.

6) *Drive* to make it want to use that speed when on the line, and which – if the line is lost – will make the hound go forward to search for it on fresh ground.

7) *Courage* so that if left behind, a hound will come through a mass of horses legs in order to get back to the rest of the pack. Courage, so that when the opportunity occurs it will catch the fox and kill it.

8) *Fox sense* is a quality that, although difficult to describe, is something which makes a hound stand out among its fellows. Hounds that have it are not clever, but they are intelligent. They find more foxes than others and they kill more than others.

9) Finally, there is today a quality which I shall call *bidability*. It is the speed with which hounds react to the demands of their huntsman. In these days of trunk roads and electric railways, it is increasingly important, and is also a matter of intelligence. Intelligence in the hound coupled to intelligence on the part

of its huntsman, so that the hound has faith in him and trusts him to help not hinder.

You may note that I have not mentioned conformation as a quality; that is because it is not one. However, for such qualities as speed, stamina, and drive to be implemented, hounds need to have both good conformation and be fit.

Having now named the primary qualities required in a hound, let us consider how the three principal types of hounds match up to that requirement. In doing so one is making a generalisation, and, like all generalisations, it stands to be denounced.

THE ENGLISH FOXHOUND This hound stands out for courage, pack sense, drive and bidability. It has plenty of stamina and speed, a good nose and uses its voice with accuracy; speaking only when its nose informs it that it may do so.

THE WELSH HOUND   A hound with considerable *joie de vivre* and a volume of cry which is often a great help to those who follow them. It has a good nose and is very persistent.

THE FELL HOUND   This hound is, perhaps, pre-eminent in the question of nose. It has remarkable stamina, plenty of drive, and is both fast and persistent. However, I believe it is also true that it lacks pack sense.

Both the Welsh and Fell hounds do, perhaps, suffer from a degree of persistence which excludes pack sense and bidability, or it could be that by concentrating on their own lines they fail to hear and take notice of others.

THE INFLUENCE OF TOPOGRAPHY   We will now come back to an earlier part of this chapter when I said that the topography varied from hunt to hunt, and that it was the balance in which the qualities were held that mattered. The value of nose is of course greater on the cold scenting ploughs of Lincolnshire than on the heather-covered slopes of our moors. The value of courage is greater in Leicestershire with 200 horsemen out and 800 legs to go through than in the deep wooded valleys of Devonshire. The value of speed is greater in a country that is easy to ride over than in one in which woods, wire and trappy conditions make it difficult for the Field to maintain contact. Hunting is a sport and there is no point in having hounds after which the Field gallop vainly shouting enquiries to find out which way they went! Hunting is a means of control, and a pack of hounds which gets further and further behind its foxes exerts no control for it invariably eventually runs out of scent. All is a matter of balance depending on local conditions and requirements.

Hound Breeding

I mentioned before that most kennels contain a cross made up of various types of hound, and that it had been the life work of a number of distinguished Masters to develop with care the crosses and lines which, in their opinion, suited them and their countries. In that statement *care* is the operative word for it is only with care that the balance is achieved to suit specific conditions, conditions which may change as the hunting country itself changes.

If we study the roots of these carefully bred hounds, we find in the pure English hound an animal which can on occasion trace its male and female pedigrees back to the early 1700s. However, those pedigrees were kept in the private pedigree books of some hunts, and it was not until 1841 that the first volume of the Foxhound Kennel Stud Book was produced. It was this fact which together with the start of the Hound Shows towards the end of the last century that began to produce a degree of standardisation which sometimes depended upon fashion rather than effectiveness for its background. The Belvoir, Brocklesby and Beaufort set standards which were no doubt right in those countries at that time, but since then those countries have changed and many others have always been different. If this was the case in England it was not often the case in Wales. There, numerous small private packs also hunted the fox, and their owners, often mounted on strong Welsh cobs, admired the cry, persistence and individual low-scenting abilities of Welsh hounds.

It was therefore fortunate that the turn of the century saw some far-sighted men hunting hounds on the Welsh borders who disapproved of some of the trends that had become fashionable. They included noticeably Mr. (later Sir Edward) Curre, who persisted in linking the tongue, nose and cry of the Welsh hound with the drive, courage, and pack sense of the English. Therefore, when in 1928 the Foxhound Kennel Studbook was closed for over thirty years, there were already hounds with the Welsh cross in recognised foxhound kennels. It was a fact which provided the opportunity for Mr. Isaac Bell to develop an animal very different from what generally existed in the thirties; animals often generally thought of as the English hound. In turn he was followed by Sir Peter Farquhar, and Captain Ronnie Wallace, who by developing Mr. Bell's and Lord Coventry's ideas, changed the foxhound from what it was then to what it often is today – a very different animal. However, nothing stands still and change has not been limited to the Welsh lines introduced generally through their Portman and Heythrop stallion hounds, and further developed by the late Duke of Beaufort.

For generations, the high Fells of Cumberland and Westmorland saw a very different form of foxhunting. Using light-bodied, active, hare-footed hounds, probably descended from the fast northern hounds of years gone by, the Fell men hunted their foxes with hounds that were fast and had good noses, and followed them on foot. Often trencher-fed, they stayed out on the farms for most of the summer, and were encouraged to be individualistic. The result was that later in the winter, foxes were often accounted for by one or two hounds hunting on their own. What could not be prevented was turned into a virtue!

Now, even as Sir Edward Curre's hounds influenced the development of the foxhound, in the years immediately before and after the last war, Sir Alfred Goodson's College Valley hounds repeated the performance with Fell blood, which was given added momentum when the Kennel Stud Book was reopened with its five generations rule.

Now as we enter the eighties, new Masters are still repeating the process. In Wales a fast new hound is being produced by crossing the Welsh hound with the Fell hound direct, while in England certain Masters have also gone direct to the Fells or to previously unused Welsh lines for fresh blood. It is an expensive process because, if the advantages are to be reaped any undesirable qualities must be ruthlessly culled. However, experimentation is usually left to the few, and most of the hounds you will hunt with have been bred with care, using other people's experience. It is, in fact, of great benefit to the foxhound that these experiments exist, and it is also a good thing that by the time the results reach most packs, the experiments lie two or three generations in the past.

However, it will be a sad day if we see exactly the same thing and the same type of hound everywhere, because, although some would benefit, others would not. The individualism that for so long has been part of the hunting scene would have gone, and much of the fun of visiting a fresh pack in fresh country would have gone with it. Standardisation is however unlikely to occur, for, as foxes, country and people change so will the kinds of hound used change with them. Indeed, if you get the chance of a few days with different packs, you will not only find it interesting but it may well influence your ideas about hunting and where you hunt in the future.

6 The Quarry

The Fox

There are numerous kinds of foxes. They vary in size and colour from the little desert foxes, through the white Arctic foxes, to the European red fox. It is this latter, or rather the variety of it that is found in the British Isles with which we are concerned, for it is this variety that is hunted with hounds more than any other animal in the world.

The weird cry of the female fox (vixen) in the long winter nights of late December and January, has for generations sent a shiver down the backs of the unknowing, who often believed that its eerie cadences foretold something evil. In fact, all that they usually do foretell is that in about two months time a litter of cubs is likely to be born.

FOX CUBS When the cubs are born, they vary in numbers from one or two to over a dozen. They are dark in colour, their eyes are closed and the males weigh about 30 per cent more than the females. They are usually born in a small earth which their mother may have enlarged from a rabbit's burrow. Such, however, are the workings of nature, that within a short space of time most litters will have reduced themselves in number to seven or less, while the weight differential results in the fox being one of the animals which has a considerable preponderance of males.

For the first month or two their mother lies in the earth with them during the day, and it is due to this fact that she will not be disturbed by hunting in March and April. She may well live in one of several earths, for foxes – unlike badgers – do not clean out their earths; instead, as one becomes soiled or attracts the unwelcome attention of dogs and people, so the foxes move to another. This sometimes results in a farmer saying that he has three litters of cubs on his farm when in fact he has one which has been moved to three places.

As the fox family grows, their mother tends to get bored with their incessant demands for food. She starts to live at some distance from the earth, somewhere from which she can watch it during short breaks in her never-ending hunt for food and the task of supplying the growing family. How difficult that task is, depends upon the size of the family and the part played by the cubs' father, this latter being variable. As with humans, there are good fathers and bad; some are a major source of supply, others appear to have given the whole thing up well before the cubs are born!

By the time the cubs lose their fluffy brown coats and develop the smooth summer coat of the red fox, they have become too heavy for the vixen to carry and so they trail behind as she moves about. While the vixen had to carry the cubs she would go on returning as long as there was another cub to carry, but when they trail behind her I believe that some vixens are satisfied if at least three cubs remain. She may go back if agitated cries reach her, or something appears wrong, but it is my belief that this is the second reason for a drop in the size of litters. The number of cubs that are found alone at this age, outside an earth or stuck in a rut or ditch, together with the fact that litters of four or five may well now become three, suggests that both the age and the number are of importance. Jaundice also takes its toll at this stage for there is no vet to provide the necessary injections.

DIET In June the cubs will begin to feed themselves. Indeed, though many people think of the fox as a purely carnivorous beast – it is not. Like man, it is omnivorous. Fresh pheasant or rabbit may be the principal foods for some families, but the dustbins of our cities, towns and villages certainly feed as many foxes, if not more. Even the most particular country foxes like their blackberries and apples in due season, and the big black beetles that frequent the cow pats are, apparently, a delicacy. Fields of roots provide great pickings for foxes – slugs, snails and mice are always there, while kale provides the roosting places for countless small birds. Then, like a poacher in a pheasant roost, a fox has only to reach up and he can help himself.

Foxes therefore tend to grow up eating what the vixen brings them up on. However, to this should be added what hunger and an insatiable curiosity provide. Thus, when a cub sees a blade of grass moving and his sharp ears hear a tiny rustle, the belly flattens, then like a coiled spring, it pounces. Its nose comes down between its feet, it bites something that it smells there – exit a mouse, enter a killer.

Thus it progresses: the fox learns that moles are all bones and not good to eat but are good to roll on, that a rat must be killed with one bite if it is not to get bitten itself, that bottles and tins may have sharp edges, and that human beings leave waste and waste may be good to eat. Indeed, by mid-July the cub is probably self-supporting, but it still lives in the same area as the rest of its family. It knows the same area, the same woods, the same tracks and perhaps the same roads and gardens. And so it will continue until it is forced to go further afield, perhaps by hounds, perhaps by hunger, perhaps by sex, perhaps by another fox.

BEING HUNTED   So we come to the period of the year when, if a fox lives in the country, the hunter may become the hunted. An animal that itself uses smell to hunt knows all about scent.

The fox is nearly full grown and is completely independent; it knows every creep and it is fit from its nightly foraging expeditions when it covers many miles. It is one of the most agile animals in the world, but it leaves behind it a strong scent which comes from its pads, body and the scent gland under the base of its brush. How quickly that scent deteriorates, spreads or finally vanishes depends upon the climatic conditions of the day and the kind of surface on which it lies; wet or dry, grass, plough or tarmac.

Matched against him, the fox will have a pack of hounds who have none of the local knowledge and whose fitness depends upon those who look after them. Hounds who are aided by a number of human beings, some of whom get in the way and are not known by the hounds; others, at most three or four, they do know and, we hope, trust. Hounds which have been bred for generations, with variable success, to catch foxes by means of sensitive noses. Who wins this contest varies, but usually some of the litter of foxes will die while the majority escape. If they die, it is very quick, with the strength of the pack bringing almost instant oblivion, or, if the fox has gone to ground, it may be the bang of a humane killer that brings the end, after the fox has been dug out with pick and shovel.

If it lives, its experience will have taught it much. It will know it is wise to get out of the way at the sound of a horn or the cry of hounds. It may well have learned how to shift hounds on to another fox by running with or behind it and then turning off at an acute angle. It may have jumped on to a wall and run cat-like along it, while hound after hound has crossed and recrossed it never pausing to own the scent on top. What is certain, is that however it has avoided the hounds on this occasion it will certainly try again next time – if it worked once, it may well work again.

The disturbance caused by a first day's hunting may well not end there, however, for it may persuade dog foxes in particular to go further afield, since their old home with its memories and smells no longer appears so attractive.

Autumn turns to winter, the general undergrowth is cut back by the first frosts. Food gets scarcer and hunting for it gets harder. It is perhaps as well that there are not as many mouths to feed as in July. An old fox, who for years has avoided hounds by sleeping in a hollow crown of an oak tree, is killed by a sheep-dog when he invades a farm yard. Thin and hungry, age has brought him no comfort, his teeth are worn, his weight is slight. However, the young foxes are fit and well, and able to look after themselves; they are nature's destroyers of the old and injured. A bird with a broken wing, a rabbit caught in a snare, a fish left flapping on the mud when a mill-leat ran dry; all provide food till the eerie cry of the vixen breaks out again, and then they will go off to start the whole cycle once more.

AGE EXPECTANCY   If the hounds do not catch him, how long will a fox live? In captivity foxes have lived into their teens, but the wild is very different from captivity. In the wild meals must be won and physical fitness is the first requirement. For a fox to live to the age of eight would be very unusual.

And what of town foxes? In the 1930s the spread of city suburbs and the resultant new sources of readily available food, encouraged the growth of the urban fox population, and the sighting of a city fox is now, as then, a more common occurrence than the sighting of its rural counterpart.

The age expectancy of an urban fox is probably less than that of its country cousin however, because, although not hunted by hounds, the dangers of the motor car, poison and disease are prevalent.

The Red Deer

The European red deer is essentially a forest animal. In Germany it is found in that country's massive fir-based forests and it is shot with a rifle, usually from a hide or platform. In France too it lives in large areas of woodland, but is usually hunted by hounds; many of the packs having their own distinctive breeds.

In Great Britain, red deer are found in two principal areas; Scotland and certain parts of the West Country, the hub of which is Exmoor. In the former, they are mostly on bare, barren ground not entirely natural to them. There they live, but they do not develop to the degree that they do in areas where there is a better and greater permanent food supply. Their numbers are controlled by stalking, the sport bringing much needed work and money to the Scottish Highlands. In the latter, the number of red deer had shrunk to a mere handful when, in 1855, Mr Bisset re-established the Devon & Somerset Staghounds. The next twenty-six years not only saw this sorry remnant develop into a substantial herd but also saw an entirely fresh herd developed on the Quantock Hills. The reasons for this being that a) poaching stopped as the local population became far more interested in the deer, and b) in the early days, the deer were not killed at the end of a hunt, but were 'taken' and transported to Mr Bisset's private estate in the Quantock Hills where they formed the nucleus of today's herd. There are now many hundreds of deer in North Devon and Somerset with a growing number in Cornwall. They are there because of the love of staghunting inherent in much of the farming population and they are also responsible for a significant element of the tourist industry, spring staghunting in particular bringing many visitors to the area.

CALVES   The hind – as the female red deer is called – usually has her calf in June. It is fawn in colour with white spots on its coat; but the calf's coat will change to the russet-brown of the red deer within a few months. June is an ideal time for the calves to be born for by then the vegetation of the moor and its surrounding woods and farmland is at its best for producing the milk that the hind must provide. Indeed, it is the improvement in the quality of this food that is the basis for the rise in the deer population that has taken place in the last fifty years.

Calves, when they are born, have one very important instinct. They will lie absolutely still when the hind is away feeding, for it is movement that attracts attention. However, sometimes someone finds an abandoned calf. If only they would leave it and watch from some distance down wind, they would usually see the abandoned one become reunited with its mother, provided of course, that the smell of human beings does not contaminate it.

ANTLERS   As the summer progresses the hind will rejoin her herd, a social group often led by an old barren female. However, they will have nothing to do with the stags who live in small groups on their own. In fact, during this period, the stags are growing their new horns or antlers. Deer, in contrast to antelope, lose these antlers each spring and then grow new ones. How they develop depends upon two things; the amount and quality of the food available, and the age of the deer. As the antlers grow they are covered with a soft furry substance, known as velvet, through which runs numerous small veins supplying blood to the growing horn. However, when the horn stops growing, the blood supply dries up and the velvet is rubbed off. The fact that it is usually rubbed off against the bark of a tree sometimes makes the enthusiastic forester the enemy of the deer, but this is seldom true when that forester is a local man who knows and understands the deer. If, however, he is part of a large company or corporation, it may be a different matter.

STAGHUNTING   The fact that stags are solitary animals, or live in small groups, greatly affects the hunting of them, for in the autumn it is only the warrantable deer, stags of five years old or more, that are hunted. They are both bigger and stronger than their younger brethren.

When found by hounds, they are in a position to do all that they can to make a younger stag run in their place – deliberately pushing one up before taking evading action. To prevent this happening, after the whereabouts and description of the stag to be hunted has been reported to the Master by the harbourer, most of the hounds will be shut up in a farm or lorry and just a few – the tufters – are taken to find the right deer and separate it from the others. This may take several hours if an old stag manages to divert the hounds on to a younger one, or otherwise give them the slip. However, eventually they should force him to go away and head for some distant part of the area he knows.

THE RUT Stag hunting lasts from early August to mid-October when the rut starts. This is the period of about one month during which the stags collect their hinds and mating takes place. During the rut, the sleek and graceful animals of the autumn become fierce, roaring creatures, their bodies black with sweat and from wallowing in the peat bogs, and gaunt from not sparing the time to feed as, unceasingly, they collect and control their hinds. Indeed, the fact that they are permanently on the move does result in changes of control, for incessant activity weakens them and provides an opportunity for smaller or weaker deer to take over. This is a natural way of spreading parentage and reducing in-breeding.

The whole process lasts for only one month, and during it not only are the next year's calves provided for but the last year's are weaned. When it is over, the fighting and mating stops and the deer once again congregate in herds, the big stags usually lying down-wind of their hinds. It is interesting at this time to visit a field where deer have been feeding – some patches will have been systematically grazed by the hinds, and in others a stag will have taken a bite here and a bite there before wandering on.

HUNTING THE HINDS AND THE YOUNGER STAGS With the calves weaned and the winter arrived, hind hunting starts and continues until mid-February. In many ways it is more skilled than stag hunting, for hinds frequently circle back to the same herd or join another and the task of sticking to the same deer can be very difficult. Finally, with the hinds' pregnancies nearing the half-way mark, hind hunting ends – there is a brief pause and then in March and April the younger two-, three- and four-year-old stags are hunted. Fit and hard after the winter, perhaps well fed as a result of the improving agriculture, they frequently produce the longest and hardest hunts. Then as April draws to its end, they too shed their horns leaving a small raw patch from which, in due course, the new horn will grow.

AGE AND POPULATION   In June when the calves are born, the stags will already be showing quite a length of new horn growth and the annual cycle starts. The size of the head usually increases until the deer is nine or ten years of age, after which, as he finds it more difficult to make the best use of his food, the size of his horns may decrease. He is then said to be 'going back' and will eventually die – perhaps killed by another stag, perhaps by man, perhaps by other natural causes.

In fact, red deer frequently live to a considerable age, some having recorded ages of over twenty. Nevertheless, as with most animals, their strength, size, and the survival rate among their calves largely depends on the food supply. In Scotland, that food supply is strictly limited and if enough deer are not killed, others will die, probably of starvation. In the West Country however, the agricultural revolution has greatly increased the food available and as a result it has also increased the size of the deer population, which, in turn, has resulted in rising damage to farm crops.

There is no doubt that the popularity of stag hunting among the farming fraternity of Exmoor not only keeps the deer alive but also keeps them in good health. Poaching, though not unknown, remains slight in the area regularly hunted. Elsewhere however, whatever the legal situation the deer are not of as much interest to the ordinary farmers and so are not cared for in the same way. Indeed, it can truly be said that the hounds are the guardians of the deer, and the fact that large numbers of them still exist in a truly wild state is largely due to the hunts; a fact that is not always appreciated.

The Hare

Hares were among the earliest animals to inhabit the British Isles. For most of that time they have been hunted by man, a fact borne out by the cave drawings and fossil evidence. However, despite this long interest, large gaps in our understanding of the species remain. Most of the basic facts are of course known, but the reasons behind their remarkable rises and falls in population, their behaviour, and the occasional mass migrations are not. At best they are guessed at, at worst their existence is not even appreciated.

HARE VARIETIES There are three varieties of hare in the British Isles. Of these, the brown hare, with a maximum weight of twelve to thirteen pounds is the largest. The Irish hare – which seldom exceeds ten pounds – is in turn usually larger than the blue, or mountain, hare whose top weight is seven pounds. However, all hares, whatever their size, are biologically largely the same. They all breed at about one year old, and usually produce from two to four small litters in each year which vary in size from one to three leverets. These are born fully furred and with their eyes open after a pregnancy of six weeks. Births take place in the spring, summer and autumn and it is probable that the actual number of litters depends upon the survival rate of those first born.

HARE BEHAVIOUR Hares are herbivores and largely nocturnal, feeding in the evening and early morning. The days are usually spent in one or other of their seats or forms. These small hollows, or scoops in the ground, are placed so that they provide the hare with a good view of the land in front and beside them. At the same time, I believe, the one chosen for occupation usually has the wind behind it. The hare can thus see one way and smell or hear the other. Despite this, hares have a tendency to try and shrink into the ground and disappear at the approach of danger; they then leave at the last moment, a fact which has a great influence on the hunting of them.

The meeting of the 'mad March hares' in the spring, though probably for mating purposes, has a social as well as a sexual background, for it is a fact that although hares produce up to four litters a year and are not monogamous, they only normally behave like this in the spring. At the same time it should be noted that considerable local migrations sometimes take place and word of an especially succulent new food supply seems to get round with no effort being made to protect it.

One of the problems in studying hares, is that they are very hard to sex. 'Puss' – as they are often called – is usually also referred to as 'she'. However, when hares have been carefully sexed, it has been discovered that there are small does as well as large, and large jacks as well as small. Personally, I think that size is decided more by the number in the litter, the food supply available and heredity, than sex.

The question of food supply is of course very important. The liking of hares for valuable crops such as sugar beet can make the farmer an enemy. Equally, a liking for the tender shoots of trees sometimes does the same with the forester. However, the speed with which land is turned over after harvest, the fact that the early cuts of silage are made when the first litters are still small, and that large numbers of hares are killed on country roads, is probably more serious in its effect on hare numbers than any deliberate effort to kill them. At the same time, I also think that agricultural disturbance when continuous, may help to bring about the mass migrations which occasionally take place.

Hares, however, die without being obviously killed. Indeed, it is unlikely that any wild hares reach the life span of ten to twelve years which they are capable of. Liver diseases, such as fluke, kill some; others have been found to suffer from diseased intestines and yet others may poison themselves. Indeed, hares do not seem to have the marked antipathy to poisonous plants shown by most animals and it is recorded that under conditions of great cold, they have been poisoned in large numbers by eating broom. Similarly, they appear to like the dead foliage of plants killed by gramoxone and it is probable that sprays are yet another non-deliberate cause of death related to modern agriculture.

HARE HUNTING Despite death and migration, hares are still found in much of the British Isles, and in most of them they are hunted by harriers or beagles. As an animal to hunt, they have far more in common with the stag than the fox. Like a stag, they tend to accelerate away and then, when well ahead, turn, twist and run their own foil before bounding to one side and again lying down or waiting. Like a stag, they will deliberately push up another to run in their place, and like a stag, they will deliberately lie still until the last possible moment; then, they will spring up and if possible race uphill leaving the hounds to toil in their wake.

The natural behaviour of hares with their inclination to circle and lie down, probably lends itself more to beagles than harriers because people on their feet are usually only too pleased to stand still and watch, while those on horses generally want to push on. However, there is nothing like the back of a sensible horse and a good pack of harriers if one wants to learn about venery.

7 Two Sets of Problems

Many people who go out hunting will see the Master and his hunt staff and secretly envy them. As a new subscriber you may know what is expected of you, however you may well not think about what is expected of them.

As a subscriber, it will be your decision whether or not you go out. If you do, you have only to get your horse ready in time to get to the meet. If it pours with rain and you are wet, cold and miserable – you can go home. Your worries are yours; they concern your horse and you. How different from the concerns of those red-coated figures. They may have personal problems but their principal worries must concern the hunt. They cannot go home if they want to and their worries must be about the organisation of the day itself and what is going to happen.

Problems for the Master and Field Master

It is the Master's task to balance the interests of his followers against the needs of his 'country'. That means that on the one hand the hounds have to hunt all their country, catching enough foxes in its various parts to keep their numbers under control. On the other, they must provide the sport and excitement that their subscribers require.

In balancing these two objects, the Master will try to see that on the days when most people are likely to be out, the pack will be in the most rideable part of the country. He will be influenced by when he was last in the area, what is traditional within the hunt as regards the general list of meets for that day in each week, and he will also be concerned about other local events. Finally, he must bear in mind the arrangements made by any shoots in the area, for it is essential that the two sports go hand in hand.

Having decided where he is going to meet, the Master will have to make sure that those who farm in the area know and expect the hounds. The earth stoppers must also know what is required of them, and if he does not hunt the hounds himself, he will also have to discuss the day with his huntsman. They will plan it in outline, leaving enough flexibility to ensure that problems created by the direction of the wind and the behaviour of the first foxes found, do not nullify the rest of the day.

Once at the meet, with the planning of the day complete, the Master may well take on the duties of Field Master. In this role he will become the arbitrator between the desires of his Field and the needs of the huntsman. It is his task to see that the Field are able to keep in close contact with the hounds and watch them; at the same time they must be prevented from putting undue pressure on the hounds. They must not over-ride them or push them off the line, and there must be room for the huntsman to take appropriate action if they check.

It will be his task to see that they get from A to B across country without abusing the farmers' hospitality. It is a difficult task and how he does it will vary from man to man. Some Field Masters will use contact or linking men, some will command, others request. Whichever they do, and however they do it, the responsibility is theirs and therefore the right to be obeyed immediately is also theirs. It must also be remembered that the job is being done at the same time as the Field Master rides his own horse across country, and that on its own is more than enough for most people.

Problems for the Huntsman

The huntsman has started his day by 'drawing' the pack he intends to hunt. Old Butterfly he leaves behind, he thinks she needs a day off. Seagull is still suffering from a wire cut on her stifle. Daphne and Pastime have had their pads cut by flints. Duchess is coming 'in season' and so on. He has talked over the day with the Master, or he will do so on the way to the meet. He knows the coverts he expects to draw, and he is concerned because the wind has moved around so that the first of them may well be disturbed by the sound of horses on the road.

Ideally, he will have two outline plans dependent on the direction of the wind and how the day starts. Few things are more frustrating for a huntsman than to find a fox at the start of a good scenting day and run through all the coverts he intends to draw in the first sixty minutes. If he does so, he will be left at midday with the choice of going where he is not expected; or he may spend the rest of the day drawing coverts already disturbed, thick hedges and odd patches of roots.

Leaving the meet, he will probably have had a guess at what scenting conditions are likely to be. Various signs may have made his guess a more informed one than that made by some members of the Field. A huntsman is glad to see some hounds eating grass at the meet, but sorry to see them rolling. He likes to see the smoke from a bonfire hang close to the ground, but is sorry to see it rising straight up into the air, and sorry to see a blue haze or cobwebs on the grass, etc. The way he approaches his first cover may be governed by that guess. Too much noise on a good scenting day, and the best fox may have left before he arrives; too little, and with a bad scent, they may draw over him or chop him before he is properly on his feet. Draw up-wind and he may surprise his fox, draw down and his whippers-in need to be in position before the noise of his approach reaches the cover.

Having arrived, the huntsman may 'put' his hounds into the cover from some distance away. Alternatively, he may walk down its edge dropping a few hounds off as he sees where the runs and tracks of small animals enter it. Which he does probably depends on the thickness of the cover; dense brambles or gorse need to be drawn with care, a hollow wood or kale require no serious penetration. The method he uses will be up to him, once again it is his decision.

As his hounds draw, the huntsman will encourage them by use of his voice and perhaps the occasional note on his horn; this lets them know where he is and gives them confidence. For the same reasons, if the cover lies on a steep bank he will usually draw it from below as hounds will invariably draw up so that they can look down on him. Hounds do not like drawing down because they may lose contact with the huntsman.

53

The next problem occurs if a fox is holla'd away. This may happen while hounds are still drawing or it may happen when they are already hunting another fox. In the first case, he will undoubtedly go to the holla, but the question is – how quick? If he gallops there as fast as he can blowing his horn, he will undoubtedly arrive there – but he will probably not have all, or even most, of his hounds. The hounds missing are likely to be his best drawing hounds and they will lose confidence in him and not draw as well next time. Equally, if he goes too slowly and waits for all and sundry, when he does arrive, the scent will be cold and an opportunity lost. It is all a matter of judgement and the speed required is the one that will get him to the holla quickly with most of his hounds.

If, however, the hounds are already hunting one fox (perhaps a small vixen who has already spent some time dodging around in thick brambles) the problem takes on another dimension. The huntsman has then to decide if he can get hold of his hounds quickly enough to make the switch worthwhile. The pack arriving in a body with their huntsman within a few minutes, gives the promise of a good hunt, but a straggling collection of hounds drifting on to the line after ten minutes or more promises nothing, and the hounds would have been far better left hunting their original quarry. It is largely a matter of confidence; confidence of the huntsman in his hounds, and the hounds in their huntsman. Confidence that they will react to him quickly, and confidence that he will increase their chances of catching a fox.

In a good hunt, there are numerous occasions when the hounds might check, and there are probably several when they will. However, on most of these occasions, they will put themselves right. Numerous things can cause a check; manure or some other over-lying scent such as sheep foil or exhaust fumes, a sharp turn by a fox when the natural drive of the hounds causes them to overshoot the line, and the tricks of the fox, such as running along the top of a wall or turning back on his own line. The moment they check, the huntsman has three problems:

1) What does he think the fox has done?
2) Does he think the hounds in their natural unaided cast will be able to regain the line?
3) Should he act, and if so when?

54

For example: the hounds check some fifty yards out in a grass field. There is no obvious reason, except that the Field were pressing on the hounds at the last fence which was both thick and wide. The huntsman thinks his fox has turned short at the fence but he has no way of knowing whether it has turned left or right. However, he has noted that on the two occasions earlier in the hunt when there was a slight change of direction, it was to the left. He cannot go back to where the hounds crossed the fence for some members of the Field are already between it and him, the steam from their horses further killing the scent. He looks at his hounds, who are spreading in an arc in front of him. There is a good chance that they will hit the line if the fox has gone on. He leaves them alone because he has made a mental appreciation of what has happened and has decided that that is the right thing to do and not because it is the easiest thing to do. His patience is rewarded. One wing of the spreading pack picks up the line and the others race to its cry. Because the hounds have done the work themselves, they will try that much harder next time, they will also settle down more quickly to the existing line. Some of the Field will think the huntsman slow, more will notice nothing except a slight hold up.

However, what would have happened if the hounds had not hit off the line? Their huntsman would not have wasted his time while hounds cast themselves. He would have watched them, but he would also have had a glance at the ground to see if there was any sign of foil, and he would have seen how the thick hedge developed as it ran on to the corner of the field. Now, having seen his hounds fail to recover the line, he decides to cast them himself. One touch on the horn and he has their attention, then with a whistle or a quiet 'come on then' he goes off towards the far hedge. Nearing it, he slows down, gets his hounds ahead of him and on his outside. Then, using himself as a pivot, he brings his hounds round in an arc with their heads down until they cross the line where the fox has turned and followed the hedge.

Then there is the problem that occurs if the hounds divide or perhaps just change foxes. In the first case it is a question of which lot to stop, in the second, whether to carry on, or to stop them and go back for the hunted fox. Again, there is no set answer, for time and circumstances bring differing factors to

55

bear. Indeed, the huntsman who is wrong is the one who does not appreciate the problem and invariably does the same thing.

Finally, there is the problem of the end. How long should the huntsman persevere with a stale line or an unenterprising fox. Is it right to dig, bolt or leave a fox that has gone to ground. Once again, the decision has to be made in the knowledge of local requirements.

Back at the kennels that evening, the huntsman will go through his hounds to see that they are none the worse for their day. Meanwhile at the Master's home, the telephone will ring. The voice at the end informs him that some thoughtless member of the Field has left a gate open with the result that two flocks of sheep have got mixed up – and that is another problem!

8 Clothes and Equipment

If you are going hunting for the first time I don't suppose you want to stand out – someone to be stared at or talked about rather than talked to. Of course, if you are a stranger, you will be recognised as such, and nothing that you may do or wear will alter the fact. However, most hunting people welcome strangers, and a stranger who does not also appear very unusual is unlikely to solicit more than normal conversation.

There is also the question of what you need to take with you and while refreshments, for instance, are a matter of choice, there are other things it is wise to add to the list.

Clothing

Your hunting clothes, in fact, should consist of one of a series of traditional combinations, although recent arguments about the kinds of hat that should be worn have complicated the situation.

Appearance is not everything, however, for it must be remembered that although cubhunting often takes place in an Indian summer, and stag hunting in the autumn and spring, the foxhunting season in most countries stretches from November to March. It is a period which consists of the five coldest and wettest months of the year, and so the clothes you require need to be both warm and able to resist all but the heaviest rain.

BREECHES Bad weather should not make you rush out to buy new heavy breeches or jodhpurs if you already possess thin nylon ones, because a good supply of thermal underwear may help. However, if you are going to start hunting regularly you should not allow a shop assistant to persuade you that what you really need is made of thin light-weight material.

HUNTING SHIRTS AND TIES Similarly, your hunting shirt needs to be warm and joined at the neck by a stud to which you

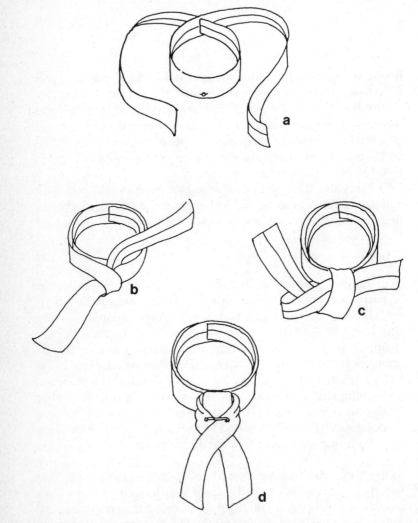

How to tie a stock. (They can also be purchased ready-tied.)

will be able to attach a stock-tie. This is a form of dress which not only keeps your neck warm but largely prevents the rain running down your back. To this may be added the advantage that a stock-tie can double as a very efficient bandage, should one be needed. A waistcoat is usually worn.

BOOTS   Long leather boots are far stronger and protect the legs better than rubber ones but price and availability play their part and should you decide to get either, do not forget that you will have socks on when you wear them and you may well have to get them off when they and you are wet through. They should therefore not be too tight a fit, and indeed there are few things as uncomfortable as a boot which starts too tight and gets tighter as the day continues.

TRADITION   You will find a list of what are virtually hunting uniforms, at the end of this section, no mention is made however of the colour of gloves. Riding gloves, which need to be warm and provide a good grip even when wet, are usually the same colour as the breeches, although some ladies with blue coats also like to wear blue gloves!

In the same lists, a distinction is made between a hunt member and a subscriber. It is a distinction which perhaps requires an explanation: anyone, other than a farmer over whose land the hunt goes, who consistently hunts with a pack of hounds, must become a subscriber to the hunt with which they hunt. For them to become members of that hunt, they would have to be invited to wear the hunt's distinctive button by its Master. Once they have been asked, they would normally remain members should the Mastership change.

The criterion used before that invitation is made, will vary from hunt to hunt and perhaps from Master to Master. In some cases those who have subscribed for a given number of seasons will automatically be asked. In others, the request follows additional work, such as that connected with the organisation of social events, the running of the point-to-point, or the rearing of hound puppies. It is also true that in most – if not all hunts – the request when made applies also to the husband or wife of the person asked.

HATS   In the old days, Masters and hunt servants were alone in wearing black hunting caps with the ribbons at the back dropping down towards the collar. Male members or subscribers wore top hats, ladies wore bowlers, or, if they rode side-saddle, top hats, and farmers wore hunting caps without the ribbons.

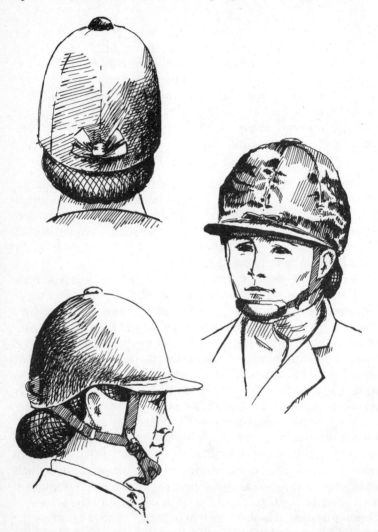

Top: Neatly netted hair. Ribbons sewn up. Middle: Skull-cap with silk. Bottom: Velvet cap with fixed safety harness.

The first break in tradition came when most ladies decided that hunting caps were more becoming than bowlers. They sewed up the ribbons and enclosed their hair in a net. However, it was not until the end of the seventies that a serious rebellion took place by the men. Then, when it happened, it was based on a series of highly publicised accidents in which top hats either came off or failed to do their job. In fact, the first organised change happened when Sir Watkin Williams-Wynn decreed that grey hunting caps might be worn, when out with his hounds, in the place of top hats.

Now it is generally accepted that anyone may wear a hunting cap or crash helmet if they so wish – however I think that it is also true that these hunting caps should not be black and thus prevent the instant recognition of status that used to exist.

Perhaps the most important thing for any hat of any type is that it is both comfortable and does not come off. It needs to be fitted with care, with the hair of the same length and cut that it will be when the hat is used. Chin harness should be worn with skull-caps. If a silk is added the colour should be that specified by the hunt.

HUNT UNIFORMS Before going on to the varying combinations of clothes which make up the different hunting uniforms, it is as well to touch on vocabulary. Most hunt servants have red coats and the members wear scarlet, they do not have pink coats or wear pink. Similarly people have a hunting whip not a crop. Crops belong to farmers or birds and a good crop for hunting is one that is likely to hold a fox!

The following lists of clothes are those traditionally worn out hunting. To all of them may be added waistcoats, and breeches and gloves whose type and colour have already been discussed. The question of hats has also been discussed, but for ease of distinction the old combinations are still kept here. However, wherever top hat is mentioned, grey hunting cap or grey covered skull-cap can be put in its place:

Masters and Hunt Servants Black hunting cap with the ribbons hanging down towards the collar. Red, green or other appropriate coloured coat, with appropriate collar and hunt button. A

Correct dress for hunt members

square cut coat with four or five buttons down the front. White breeches. Black boots with mahogany tops and white garter straps; spurs. White stock with plain gold pin.

An ex-Master Still a Member of the M.F.H.A.   The same as above except that a black coat replaces a red or green one.

Hunt Member (male)   As above, except top hat (note initial remark). Red coat, rounded front, three or four buttons *or* swallow-tail coat and light (champagne) top to boots *or* black coat and black top boots.

Hunt Member (lady riding astride)   Bowler hat or hunting cap with ribbons cut or sewn up (hair contained neatly in a hair net). Black or blue coat with appropriate collar and buttons. Light coloured breeches. Black boots and spurs – no top to the boots. White or cream stock-tie and plain gold pin.

Hunt Member (lady riding side-saddle)   Top hat, hunting cap or bowler hat with veil. Black or blue coat and habit, hunt buttons. White stock-tie and plain gold pin. Black boots and single spur.

Farmer   Black hunting cap without ribbons. White stock-tie. Black coat (with three or four hunt buttons if appropriate). Fawn brown or drab breeches. Black boots and spurs – no top to the boots.

Subscriber   As for hunt member except that hunt buttons may not be worn – while a bowler hat, black coat, drab breeches and black boots may.

Rat-Catcher (men and women)   Bowler hat or hunting cap with ribbons cut. Coloured or white stock-tie with pin or collar and tie. Whipcord or tweed coat, usually brown or greenish. Fawn or drab breeches. Black or brown boots and spurs.

Other than with foxhounds, red or scarlet coats should never be worn by anyone except Masters and hunt servants. With

Rat-catcher – traditionally worn for cubhunting

Correct dress for children
Top: small children may disperse with the thong of the whip in the interests of safety.
Bottom: spurs should not be worn by children or inexperienced riders.

staghounds, only black coats or rat-catcher are worn. Rat-catcher is also usually worn during cubhunting or after April 1st.

Equipment

When you list what you should take with you out hunting, the list divides naturally into two. First, there is what you actually take with you on your horse, and then there is what remains behind in your car or horsebox.

WHIPS AND POCKET KNIVES   Perhaps the most obvious is a whip. You should have a hunting whip, one with a strong bone or horn handle with which you can hold a gate open or pull one shut. It should also have a loop at its other end by which the thong and lash are attached. The hunt staff may on occasion use the whip to stop or turn hounds, but you are far more likely to use it to persuade the hounds to keep clear of your horse's legs.

Another important use of the thong is to form a loop at the end of the whip, by this means a horse that has had a fall and lost its bridle may be recaptured and returned to its owner. However, it is true that an increasing number of people take out riding whips rather than hunting whips. It is a habit which, though reasonable from a riding point of view, shows little consideration for anyone else.

A second important item is a pocket knife, which, with a piece of string, can often produce temporary repairs to saddlery.

FOOD AND DRINK   However, there are many people who would put sustenance above a knife, and indeed, a flask and sandwiches can be very important on a bad day! In fact, there are two types of flasks; the larger ones which are kept in a case attached to your saddle, and pocket flasks, which, personally, I dislike, having once broken some ribs on one, however they may be better for your reputation than a more obvious attachment to your saddle! Sandwiches or chocolate are another asset, but they too are far better in a pocket from which they can be easily taken out, and to which they can be quickly returned.

SPARE GLOVES   Many people find it useful to have a spare pair of gloves with them in case of loss or damage to the original pair.

The remaining equipment, which is left in the horsebox, comprises a number of important items. You will of course have taken a head collar, sweat rug and hay net for your horse. You will also have taken some refreshments and a warm coat for yourself, but there are some other items which it is a good idea to have as well – though you are unlikely to need them.

FIRST AID AND FARRIERS TOOLS   First and foremost comes a first aid box containing bandages, liniment, plaster, scissors and the means whereby an open wound can be cleaned. Next comes a hoofpick, hammer and a pair of farrier's pinchers, as a spread or twisted shoe may need removing. Many horses have been lamed because a twisted shoe has not been removed in time.

SPARE TACK   Finally it is a good idea to have a spare rein, girth, and stirrup leather in the horsebox. If you break any of them early on in the day, part of that day will probably be lost, but there is no reason why it should all be. Indeed, in former days, second horsemen usually had a spare stirrup leather as part of their uniform.

9 Behaviour in the Hunting Field

If you decide to go hunting you will do so because you hope to enjoy yourself. However, if you expect enjoyment from the hunt, what is it entitled to expect from you?

Good Manners

I have already stated that if you intend to hunt regularly with any pack, you will need to subscribe to it. You will also probably have to pay a daily levy or Field money. Alternatively, if you just have an odd day there will be a daily 'cap' to pay. However, money is by no means all that is expected of you, for of more importance are good manners. Good manners within the hunt that you are joining and good manners to people outside the hunt. In particular to your hosts; the farmers on whose land you ride.

If you join a golf or tennis club you will enjoy yourself on land that belongs to that club. If you have a gun in a shooting syndicate, you will rent the relevant rights on the land you shoot over, but if you go hunting you will spend the entire day riding over other people's land, and the reason you are there is because of the generosity and sporting traditions of those who control it.

That generosity however can sometimes be stretched by unreasonable behaviour. Of course, some damage and inconvenience can always be caused when a number of people ride across country, and that inconvenience is likely to be proportionally greater where the farms are small. However, because of the relationship between the hunt and the local community, that damage can usually be put right to everyone's satisfaction, and it is only when people are thoughtless that the relationship breaks down.

If stock are let out when a gate is left open, if the milk lorry fails to get through due to the road being blocked, or if the farmer – who is, after all, your host – is ignored then he, rightly, gets angry. It may be that this happens because he is not recognised in the hurry of the moment, but it costs nothing to say 'good day' or 'thank you', and there has to be time to make sure that stock are secure. Indeed the motto 'do unto others as you would be done by . . .' should be engraved on every foxhunter's heart.

Politeness of course also applies within the hunt itself. The normal civilities of acknowledging the Master on arrival at the meet and of finding the secretary to pay your cap, rather than waiting for him to find you, are easily done. However, of equal importance is the treatment of your fellows. Every year a few people get hurt because they get jumped on or kicked by other members of the Field. You need to see someone, directly in front of you, land safely before finally committing yourself at a fence.

You need to see someone land safely before committing yourself at a fence

There is no excuse for galloping on while someone tries to remount after having closed a gate.

There is no excuse for galloping on while a solitary individual vainly tries to shut a gate or hops about trying to get on – having dismounted to do so. Even worse is the person who brings out a horse he knows will kick, or the puller he can only stop by running into the person in front. A red ribbon on the tail of a horse that kicks may be a warning sign, but it excuses nothing. Then there is the politeness of time. If the advertised time for the hounds to meet is 11 a.m., followers should be there by 11 a.m. What is more, they should have given themselves and their horses enough time to hack on the last two or three miles. Both will feel better for the exercise and both will have settled down. However, the really important factor is that the Master's plans for the day will not be thrown into chaos by people arriving late and heading the first fox as they go to the cover side late.

Finally, good manners also dictate good manners socially.

Most hunts receive a considerable part of their income from social events run on its behalf – it is therefore important for all followers to mix together. Members, subscribers and foot followers are all part of the hunt and each needs to know the other.

The Art of Riding to Hounds

In the old days, the ability to ride to hounds was a great art. In each hunting country there were a few people who were acknowledged as being the best. That situation is no longer true as in many countries the Field is directed as well as strictly controlled by the Field Master. This gentleman is appointed partly because of his ability to give people a lead across country, partly because of his knowledge of hunting, and how much room is required by both the hounds and their huntsman, and partly because of his knowledge of the land to be hunted over and the wishes of its owners. The balance between these three things varies both from hunt to hunt and from individual to individual.

However, there are still some hunts where individual ability is important. On the whole, they tend to be at both ends of the financial scale. Some, such as the Quorn, have good grass countries which can be fairly crossed. Others are in the wilder parts of Great Britain and they are based on moorland or the old turf of the traditional stock rearing areas. In such places, an eye for the country, the ability to save your horse, and to go where you need to when you want to is still important. What does it involve?

I think that there are in fact three main reasons why some people can do this and others cannot. The first of these is that those who can do it are always paying attention, not to what their horse is doing or to what their neighbour is saying, but to the hounds themselves. It gives them time. They are able to anticipate what will happen and so can get into the right position. With time on their side they are not in a hurry and can look ahead. Time gives good horsemen the opportunity to make the best use of their horses; knowing what they think will happen, they also have to have sufficient confidence in themselves to act on it.

71

Let me explain: if you are paying attention, you notice which way the wind is blowing. You see where the huntsman has taken his hounds to draw and you notice where the whipper-in has gone in the hope of seeing the fox away. As a result you will be in the right position when the ecstatic notes of the horn announce that the fox has gone. You will also have had a good look around the field you are in, and you will know exactly how you can get out of it whichever way the hounds go.

A good horseman will walk rather than canter when he can, and he will also canter rather than gallop. By paying attention he will have saved time, and by saving time he can save his horse. Because he knows where he is going he will not over-face it. A horse going well out hunting will continue to go well. A horse who is over-faced and frightened once will be over-faced that much more easily next time.

Then there is that tantalising phrase 'an eye for a country', what does it mean? Perhaps it has connections with those abilities, already discussed, to anticipate and ride. However, there is also the ability to know exactly where you are at any one time and where everything else is too, including nearby coverts or earths; but there is more to it than that. Possibly the most important quality is that of detailed and accurate observation, and to this must be added a fair amount of animal understanding.

Not only do the best men and women who ride to hounds follow them with due regard for the land they are on, they also anticipate their moves, hoping to be on the inside of any turn they make, and then there is one final quality – courage. Courage to jump what has to be jumped even if it looks like a fall. Courage to make your own decision and the courage to carry it through.

10 An Imaginary Day's Foxhunting

Having got this far, it may be of interest to provide the reader with an imaginary day's hunting with both foxhounds and staghounds. Days that never took place but are nevertheless typical of many that do. However, here there is a problem as no day is the same for everyone. The huntsman, the Field Master, a seasoned member and the occasional visitor all look at it from different points of view and their memories of it will be different too. If hounds check in a grass field, the huntsman may remember his annoyance that the Field were too close for him to cast back to the previous fence – the Field Master will wonder if that small group on the left flank have in fact crossed the line and whether there is a gap in the fence out of the field in which Mr Jones' cattle are being wintered. The seasoned member will no doubt be hoping that the pack will soon run on over an area that his knowledge of the country informs him is all grass and very rideable. Finally, the visitor may be thinking about what he has seen, what he has jumped, and how he has got on with his horse. I therefore propose to divide the day's foxhunting into three sections; each part being seen from a different angle.

To set the scene: the visitor had gone to stay with a friend who hunts with the 'Blankshire'. He, having two horses, kindly offered to lend her one. As a member, he is allowed to have a limited number of guests each season, and he has therefore contacted the secretary and made arrangements for her to come out on this particular Saturday in January.

The Blankshire hunt on three days in each week. On Tuesdays and Thursdays they are on the Downs, a misnomer for the large arable farms that now cover the rolling chalk hills in the east of the country. On Saturdays they hunt in the vale, where the dairy farms still mean that most of the land is down to grass. Thorn fences divide the fields, each with a ditch on at least one side. The coverts too, which were mostly planted in the 100 years before the last war, are also based on thorn. Eight to twenty acres in size, they are usually split by a single ride, or in the case of the larger ones, two crossed rides. Before Christmas, the vale also contains a number of temporary covers, as most of the farms have at least one field of kale. The result is that the area required by the pack for each day's hunting increases as the season proceeds, as the kale is eaten and the amount of cover grows less. In fact, by mid-January it probably means that twelve or more square miles must be 'cleared' for each day's hunting, half as much again as the area required in November.

The Visitor

As the visitor drove to the meet in the horsebox, her host gave her most of this information, plus a good deal more about some of the people she was likely to meet. They had left the house with plenty of time to spare, and were able to leave their horsebox about three miles from the village of Wittington. It gave them time to hack on, and time for she and her horse to settle down and adjust to each other.

When they arrived, both the hounds (a bitch pack) and some of the followers were gathered in the forecourt of the Star and Garter, a large inn, well sited at a cross roads in the middle of the village. They politely acknowledged the Master, who also acted as Field Master, then they looked around to see who was who and what was what. The host introduced his guest to the secretary and the necessary cap was paid. She moved off to talk to an acquaintance of the evening before, at the same time she pulied up her girths ready for the day ahead.

The huntsman gave a note on his horn. The Master indicated which way the hounds would go and a channel opened up through the Field as riders rapidly got their horses out of the way. The hounds moved off led by a whipper-in with their huntsman in the centre. Behind them the Field wheeled into place behind the Master and with a clatter of hooves, the whole cavalcade moved off up a small by-road. A late arrival, meeting

A late arrival . . . backed his horse into a hedge, held out his whip and let the thong fall . . .

the hounds in the road head-on, stopped, backed his horse into a hedge, held out his whip and let the thong fall so that as the hounds passed they wheeled around it keeping well away from his horse's legs.

After about a mile, the hounds turned off into a farm lane. The cavalcade stopped and someone struggled with a gate. When it opened, the huntsman and hounds went through while the Field waited – their horses impatient – until the 'opener' remounted. Then everyone cantered on. 'Gate, gate please' – the chant went back down the line. Two people wearing rat-catcher and liberally festooned with string, stopped to shut it. They were the gate-shutters. At the start of the day they were in their place at the back of the Field but later on, if the Field split up, they would not be behind any particular section.

The huntsman put his hounds into the cover while the Field remained with its Master on the sloping ground above the wood. The visitor waited on the edge of that field where she could see what was happening. The huntsman had entered the covert, once his hounds had gone in, and his voice rose and fell as he encouraged them to draw. She could see a whipper-in standing on point at one corner of the wood, but the two farmers who had also gone on, were out of sight.

In fact, the hounds did not find, for it was only a few minutes before a holla screeched out its information from far away to the left. Within seconds she was in the middle of galloping horses, mud flew and the odd person seemed somewhat out of control. The Field Master held up his hand, his Field packed behind him, some waiting quietly, others edging this way and that. Inside the wood, the horn doubled, its quick pulsating notes bringing excitement to both man and beast. Soon the huntsman was out and within moments the voices of the hounds came back.

The Field Master had held the Field up at the corner of the covert, but now he slipped through the gate into the next field. Once through, it was easy to see why he had waited where he had for the green blades of winter wheat sprouted up from the heavy clay. It was a case of 'single file in the ditch' and the visitor found herself about number fifty in a queue of over 100. In due course she jumped the next fence, a small but solid hunt-jump with a badly poached take off and landing. She galloped on after the man in front in a mad chase of follow-my-leader.

In the next fence, two poles stuck up into the air, at the top of each was a board painted red on the outside and white on the inside. They warned that there was wire in the fence but that it was safe between the poles on the inside.

Two more fences and the Field came to a halt. The Field Master had stopped, his upraised hand once again indicating that others should do the same. In front of him the pack and their huntsman had checked. They worked their way along a fence while a bunch of cattle glowered at them from a corner, kept there by the whipper-in and two farmers.

Moving down the line of the fence, the leading hounds picked up the line, pushed through it and spoke. The others quickly went to the cry, and, slowly at first, then at a steadily increasing pace, the pack took up the line and ran on.

Master (Field Master)

Meanwhile the Field Master was worried. He had quite a large Field out and it was therefore unfortunate that the hunted fox was taking the line it was. If it continued in this direction it would soon be in the market gardens that ran along the back of Wittington. However, what to do then lay in the future, for the present he watched the hounds.

As they picked up the line, he saw a group of young farmers edging forward on the right flank. He shouted to them to 'hold hard' and 'let them settle'. He didn't like shouting but sometimes it was necessary. Then, as the pack began to increase its pace, he too moved off, cantered down and jumped the fence in the corner followed by the Field; as he galloped up the slope beyond, a loose horse thundered past, its reins flying, its saddle on one side – no doubt the product of a loose girth. When the pack checked on the edge of Wittington, the Master sent a farmer forward to have a word with his huntsman. The latter immediately picked up his hounds and – after an unsuccessful backward cast – took them out on to the road. The next draw was to be in Mr. Roberts' kale.

As both pack and Field trotted along the road, they kept to the left of the central line. Behind them a host of car followers strung out the procession. It was a fact which enabled traffic going in the opposite direction to pass easily, but was frustrating to anyone behind the hunt who was not following.

It was a situation that worried the Master. He did not like his hunt causing problems on the road and would get off it as soon as possible. All too clearly he remembered when a car driven by an angry person had killed a hound that had for a moment crossed the white line. The result had been unpleasant for everyone and a young bitch of great promise was dead.

Fortunately, they were soon off the road; down a farm lane they went, across a few fields and they were by Mr. Roberts' kale. In October there had been nearly fourteen acres of it, now only four remained.

Once again, the huntsman encouraged his hounds to go through the thick thorn fence into the kale. Two yelps indicated that the electric fence between what was eaten and what was not, was still switched on. A single hound spoke, others joined in, and the cry crescendoed as they came towards where the Field stood on the adjacent grass. A small fox popped through the fence, saw the Field and turned back in. The leading hounds came through, overshot the turn and went silent. Inside the kale there was a grumble. Some hounds spreading in their efforts to get through the fence had quickly met and killed their quarry.

The huntsman got off his horse, went through the fence and emerged with the limp, dead body. Once back on the grass, he threw the body to the pack while the quavering notes of the horn informed every one of the kill.

The Master had meanwhile been told that there was a bad gap in the fence where the hounds had checked in the first hunt. The gate-shutters had done their best to mend it, but if the cattle were not to get out something more should be done. He rode over and spoke to the hunt terrier man who got into his Land-rover and drove off.

The Huntsman

For the huntsman, the day had not gone to plan. The Star and Garter was a good meet, but the fox from Hangmans Wood had returned to the village. The one from Mr. Roberts' kale was chopped and hounds had not found in Mr. Wilson's withy-bed (willow bed) for the first time that season. Now, at nearly three o'clock on a short winter's day, he hoped that Parsons Thorns would hold. It was normally a sure find but you never knew. He sent his whipper-in on with two farmers to watch the far side.

The wind, which had got distinctly colder in the last half hour, faced the hounds as the huntsman put them into the thorns. He himself went into the covert by a little hand gate and started to move down the ride.

His voice sounded shrill to the waiting field as he encouraged his hounds to 'lieu in there' or 'rouse him up'. It was not what he said that mattered, it was the confidence his voice gave to the hounds; they knew where he was and that they were moving in the right direction.

A single 'ough' sounded in the thicket. 'Hike, hike, hike' was the instruction given as he recognised Target's voice and knew the old bitch was to be trusted. Others joined in. The chorus crashed out. They were together; all was well. An ear-splitting scream announced that a fox had left, but the pack was running hard, nothing could be done. A vixen came into the ride, ran a few yards down it and crossed over. The huntsman was there in a flash, waited for a few moments and then as the leading hounds spilled out on to the ride, he had them. He doubled his horn, rode down the ride, through the gate and across the field to where his whipper-in's hat pointed down the hedgerow, and twenty couple feathered, settled and raced away three or four minutes behind their fox.

The Field, who had been held up till the quick repetitive notes of the 'gone away' came back to them, settled down to ride. Glancing at the fence in front, he noted that an overhanging tree had killed the undergrowth in one place, making the fence easy to see and easy to jump.

The minutes rolled by; the hounds ran on always bending towards the left, until, instead of going up-wind, they were in fact running across it, heading for the hills in the distance.

The huntsman, whose eyes were on his hounds, when not looking for his own way ahead, landed in a grass field. His hounds had stopped running, no longer did their voices come back. Instead, they spread in an arc as they swung in their own cast. He looked about him. At one end of the field a boy was shutting a gate as his tractor ticked over. A few minutes ago he would have been in the middle of the field. It was time for a quick cast. Calling his hounds, he jumped out of the field where he had jumped in, and turned down the fence. He was right, for the sterns waved and with a surge the pack was running again.

Two fields further on, the pack turned again and once more the hounds headed for the hills. The fox had obviously some specific haven in mind, and he made a mental note that a forward cast would usually be the right one.

The time spent at the last check, although brief, had taken

some of the pace out of the hunt, but the pack was still going fast enough for most horses, one of which came galloping past. Its owner had seen a weak place in the last fence, forgetting that a weak place is often also a treacherous one. In this case a piece of rusty wire had brought disaster. He turned his own horse in order to ride the loose horse off. A loose horse amongst his hounds might injure them and would certainly upset their concentration.

A few more fields, and withies showed the course of a stream. On the far bank another covert could be seen. The drain at its corner was stopped, and, as he jumped the stream where a pollard willow showed a firm bank, he wondered if that was his fox's objective. The hounds' voices sounded clearly in the cover but faded as they left, still heading for the hills. They ran in two lots now, those nearest to him certainly had the most cry but he saw that most of his oldest and best hounds were with the others. A word to his whipper-in and the nearest ones were eased off their line and galloped on to their sisters.

At the base of the hills, a road ran along the edge of the vale. As the hounds neared it the huntsman could see a line of stationary cars pulled up on the verge, some of which still had their engines running, clogging the area with exhaust fumes. The hounds checked. It was a moment for the huntsman to act quickly, but how? A number of questions raced through his mind. How long had the cars been there? How far was he behind the fox? Had it had time to cross the road, or had the cars, or followers, headed it? A sharp question to one of the followers produced the answer that they had been there for under five minutes. He guessed that the fox had gone on, so he slipped the bitches through the hedge into the fields beyond, then turning with them, he kept them on his left as he moved down the road.

They picked up the line inside the first gateway and turned up towards the Downs. Now however, it was slow persistent hunting with the pack frequently needing to be edged on while keeping their heads down. Corn replaced grass as walls or wire replaced fences in most fields. A sinking sun added to the hazards of each obstacle.

The huntsman, with a failing fox in front, but with the scent dying on his hounds, watched them as they crested the hill. To lift them would be fatal unless he got them close to their fox. His eyes scanned ahead. Others might look to their horses, he looked at his hounds and for his fox. There – on the next slope he saw it – two magpies dipping; chattering and dipping. His soul leapt, for beneath them the fox, their fox, moved on; its back arched, its brush down. Out came the horn, and, with his hounds' heads up, he galloped them on hoping for a view. He slowed down fifty yards from where he had last seen the fox. The hounds' heads came down and before the fifty yards were up, they were running. On over the final ridge they ran, and down the steep side of a bank. They stopped, swung round and they roared at a hole!

The visitor got off her horse her limbs stiffening, her mind filled with a glorious confusion of incidents. She loosened her horse's girths and called to her host that it had been wonderful. It was a word she was to use over and over again to describe her day.

The Master got off his horse smiling, happy that he and his Field had had a good hunt, and happy that a day that had started so badly had finished so well. He wondered about what damage had been done and thought about how it should be put right, and who needed seeing; when and how.

The huntsman also got off and joined his hounds as they marked their fox to ground. He was the only one who could have wept, not because he had anything against the fox, for at any other time he would have done a great deal to help it, but now it was a contest – he and his hounds against the fox. This time the fox had won, by what he would always think of as foul play. It had been a good hunt; a five and a half mile point (eight miles as hounds ran) of one hour and twenty minutes.

If it had not been for the vixen at the start, the tractor, or the cars on the road, they would have won. As it was, all that they could do now was to go home. The long doleful notes on the horn said 'good night'. Those that remained wished each other 'good night'. The day was over, and they wended their way down towards a farm whose twinkling lights bade them welcome. There, cars would come, lifts would be given and arrangements made.

Twenty minutes later, up on the Downs, all was silent. The dog fox came to the entrance of the earth. He breathed in the cold night air, stretched and trotted off.

81

11 An Imaginary Day's Staghunting

Like its predecessor, this day's hunting did not in fact take place, but the places exist, and every incident described has and does take place time and time again.

It was a Saturday morning in mid-September. The first pale streaks of dawn lit up the sky and the river mist rose from the valley, or combe, as it is known on Exmoor.

The harbourer stood by his horse, looking across the valley to where a field of roots could just be seen on the skyline. Local people had told him that a bunch of five stags were feeding there regularly. A trip around the field the previous afternoon had revealed that they were three young and two older or warrantable stags. The slot, or foot, marks of the latter had showed wide and blunted at the toe in the damp soil. He was hoping to see the deer as he scanned the field with his binoculars. The sun rose behind him and, in luck's way, he just made out the dark forms grazing. Suddenly, one appeared on the bank top, jumped down and walked slowly down towards where Longwood still lay dark in the combe below. One by one the others followed, each appeared on the top of the bank for a moment and then effortlessly jumped out into the field towards him. Through his binoculars, he could see the heads of the two big deer. The larger one had an inspiring set of horns: on both sides there were three points on the main beam, brow, bey and trey, or, as is usually said 'all his rights'. In addition, at its top the horn divided on one side into two points and on the other into three. The other stag had only four points on each horn – brow, trey and two a-top; but the horns were exceptionally long and narrow, showing age.

When the deer entered Longwood, they disappeared from

An inspiring set of horns
a) two a-top (other side three a-top)
b) trey
c) bey
d) brow

sight. The harbourer remained where he was, letting his glasses range over those edges of the wood that he could see. He gave the deer time to settle down, and then went to the far end of the wood near Heasley Mill and checked the still damp ground for slot marks. There were none, and he was finally sure that they had not left. He went back to watch, lest they should be disturbed before the meet by a cattle dog or unofficial harbourer.

At eleven o'clock, the staghounds met at Sandyway. The Masters and hunt servants wore scarlet, the hunt secretary wore black with a red collar, and everyone else wore rat-catcher. There were over 200 riders, perhaps forty were visitors, many of whom had brought their own horses to Exmoor for a brief visit, others had hirelings. There were also a vast number of motor cars and the consequent crowd of foot followers.

The harbourer arrived at the meet shortly before 11 a.m. and rode up to one of the Masters. The two of them joined the huntsman and a brief discussion took place. After five minutes the hounds moved off down the road, through a gate and out over the open moor. The moorland sheep bounced away on either side and the rough hill cattle started up, moved out of the way, and looked back at the crowd of riders moving quickly by. It was not until they got to Longstone Wells that they stopped. The tufters were separated from the rest of the pack and, while most of the hounds remained at the farm with the whipper-in, the huntsman took the tufters – four and a half couple of old hounds – off to the bottom of the combe. With him were a few experienced people, but the majority of the Field followed the Master to a large grass field at the wood's edge; the same field over which the stags had returned five hours earlier.

The huntsman began to draw the wood from near the Mill. Longwood, as the name implies, is a long narrow wood; it lies on the steep side of the combe that runs up towards the open moor. Therefore, by drawing the wood from the bottom, the huntsman hoped to force his stag out on to that moor. He moved slowly, the small number of hounds quietly working their way forward. He saw one stop and turn aside; it pushed its way into some thick undergrowth following the faint scent from the early morning. Its voice rang out and, with a crash, a deer left the undergrowth. It was one of the younger stags. A few long, drawn-out notes informed the tufters that they should not continue and these were backed up by the crack of a whip. The Field watched with interest as the young stag left the cover and jumped the bank at the end of the field they were in. Five feet of solid earth with two strands of wire was treated with the contempt a supreme athlete reserves for the common-place.

Hounds were soon running again and this time the hurried notes of the horn proclaimed that it was one of the big stags, but then the crack of a whip announced that he had shifted his responsibility on to the shoulders of another. He had been seen to push up a smaller deer and then, with a bound, sink himself in to thick cover. He was still there when the hounds returned, and this time there was no shifting of responsibility. The stag ran up the valley and up the steep climb to the open moor. Once there, the tufters ran on until it was certain that the deer was away and would not return; they were then stopped. Handkerchiefs were waved, the horn blown, and the rest of the hounds were sent for. Meanwhile the stag galloped on heading into the wind that always seems to blow on the high moors; it cooled him, and his nose searched for the fresh deer he hoped to find.

With the pack taking twenty minutes to arrive, the stag had a good start. As he went, the sheep grazing on the moor started up, ran a few yards, stopped and continued grazing. Over the moor he went, over the county boundary watched by the car followers on the Withypool/North Molton road. On into Sherdon Water, where the swirl of the stream cooled his legs and refreshed him. Out of the stream and on past Wintershead to the river Barle and down that turbulent water, then out and up into the cool of the Picketstones Plantation.

Far behind him, the hounds picked up the scent and started to run. Unlike foxhounds, they were soon strung out in single file, while on either flank a host of horsemen surged forward like the bow wave of some multi-coloured boat. The pace dropped each time they came to sheep and thick bracken beds. Only the old experienced hounds knew how to force their way through the bracken, leaving a path for the Field to follow; down the steep drop into Sherdon Water. The Field split up as they followed the narrow paths down the side of the combe, and by the time the hounds were crossing the big grass fields of Wintershead the line of horsemen was strung out over several miles.

When the hounds came to the Barle they divided, some plunged in and crossed the river, others tried down nearer the bank. The two lots, watched by their huntsman, quietly worked their way down stream. When those on the far side hit the line where the stag had left the river, they turned up into the trees, sterns waving. Once there, their voices again rang out, for the scent lay stronger on the soft earth, and the trees themselves seemed to magnify the sound.

The Field, who waited by the river, expected to see the stag, but after a brief pause it was clear that he had gone on through the enclosed fields to Honeymead Cross, jumping the gates as he came to them. Indeed, all the watchers by the river saw was a small herd of hinds with their calves, which, worried, left the wood, paused and moved on.

The hounds moved on through the fields heavy with sheep

foil. Hunting steadily they were still well behind their stag which enabled the Master and some of the Field to catch up. They crossed the Exford/Simonsbath road and headed down into the Exe, just above, where, as a small stream, it leaves the moor behind.

Having reached the river, the hounds again divided. They first tried up it, but there was no scent on the water, and so, turning again, they worked their way down. They passed the little stream that tumbles its way down Ramscombe, but there was still no scent. Where the river finally leaves the moor, a barrier prevents cattle from wading up stream from the fields below. Just below it a heron rose from the river bank. The presence of this shy bird made the huntsman certain that he had left his deer behind him. A note on the horn and his hounds' heads came up. This time he tried up the Ramscombe stream. The hounds spoke where the stag had briefly left the water where a fence crossed it. On they went, not speaking until finally they picked up the line where the stag had left the stream. Then they spoke and slowly worked out the now stale line up the side of the combe, cheered on by their huntsman.

The stag had lain down in the bracken near the head of Ramscombe. He had been there for over an hour, when he first saw and heard the hounds turn up the stream away from the Exe. The sweat on him had cooled, his breathing had steadied, yet he did not move. He flattened his head on to the ground and laid his horns back.

When the first hound pushed its way through the bracken and saw the stag, it stepped back. The stag jumped up and made a dash at the hound, who, as it avoided the flashing horns, roared defiance. The stag turned and raced up the steep incline and so gained a start, but this time there was no twenty minutes advantage. Behind him both the horn and the hounds raised a furious clamour. Ahead of him other stags moved on as he crossed the wet ground, but they were fresh and he was not, so he peeled off and went down over West Pinford to the stream below. The hounds turned after him, and behind the hounds the few horses that were left followed the cattle tracks out over the wet ground where the cotton grass grows. Down he went, with, once again, the stream swirling and curling around his legs, down into Badgworthy where the hounds saw him – and there he turned to face these modern wolves, these natural foes of his heritage.

He stood up to his chest in water, his head held back ready to thrust at any that might come too near. There he stood when the first men arrived, one of whom carried a gun which was taken out of its case, loaded, and with a careful shot at twenty feet brought an end to his life. A life which had been tolerated for years that he might be hunted, a life uncaged and free. Free from human shackles and free from injury.

His body was pulled from the river by willing hands – the insides went to reward the hounds, the slots to followers to remind them of a great hunt, the meat to the farmers around Longwood whose crops had helped to make it, and his spirit? Well, that is conjecture, but I tend to think that the spirits of the wild deer of Exmoor are like the water in its streams: clear, free and wild. I think that they have little in common with those animals one sees in zoos and parks – nor do I think that they would wish it otherwise.

12 The Cost of Hunting

It is difficult to say what it will cost you if you decide to start hunting. Costs vary from country to country as well as from year to year. There is a breakdown of approximate costs at the end of this chapter.

In 1987 hunts spent sums which varied from about £15,000 to ten times that figure and this obviously resulted in differences in the required subscriptions. These in fact usually range from about £100 to £1,000.

Your subscription is not, however, your principal outlay; buying and keeping your horse is. The cost of buying it depends upon its age, ability and where you buy it. It is advisable to have suitable insurance. Keeping a horse can be very expensive depending on whether you look after it yourself or have it at livery. There is also the question of expenses resulting from visits by or to the vet, the farrier, the saddler, and the cost of your own clothes.

Then there is transport. It is a sad fact that in 1988 few roads are safe to ride on after dark. The idea of hacking home in the gathering dusk after a long day's hunting is no longer practical, and the cost of transport for both you and your horse is now a must in most areas.

Finally, there is an unspecified sum: it is the cost of the normal social membership of the hunt. Going to the point-to-point, hunt ball and other social events. It is a sum which can be large or small, but it is worth remembering.

Breakdown of Hunting Costs

(All prices quoted are approximations based on figures available in 1989.)

Hunter – £1,000–£6,000

Tack – £500–£750

Trailer – £1,000–£2,000

Horse box – from £2,000

It is possible to economise by buying good secondhand tack and transport.

Livery – stabled for 9 months – from £40 per week
     – three months at grass – from £20 per week

Shoeing – £200 per year

Veterinary fees – £150–£200 per season

Insurance – Premium for slaughter or permanent loss of use:
     7.5 per cent of the horse's value for a 75 per cent return
     9.5 per cent of the horse's value for a 100 per cent return
    – Premium for death by accident, disease etc.: 4.5 per cent of the horse's value
    – Premium for accident or external injury: 2.5 per cent of the horse's value.

Hunting clothing – from £400, depending on the quality.

Glossary of Hunting Terms

ALL HIS RIGHTS (See Antlers.)

ANTLERS (OR HORNS) Deer, unlike antelope, lose their antlers or horns each year. In Scotland, and in most places where the deer are stalked, they are referred to as antlers; in the West country they are known as horns. They have a number of points on each antler which helps to indicate the deer's age. The points are: brow, bey, tres and three a-top. A stag with all these points on both sides is said to have 'all his rights' and three a-top. There are a number of oddities such as a switch: a stag whose horns are going back or not developing as much as they once did, and a knot: a stag who has a calloused growth instead of horns or antlers – an old stag with no obvious horns.

BABBLE A hound that babbles is one who speaks when not on the line of its quarry; usually caused by excitement. A puppy may be excused babbling early in its first season, but it is a bad fault if it continues to do so after it has 'entered'.

BAY A deer goes to bay at the end of a hunt when it turns to face the hounds. It usually has its back to a formidable obstacle and keeps the hound at bay by the use of its horns. (Also see Tongue.)

BEY (See Antlers.)

BITCH PACK A pack confined to bitches.

BOLT A fox is bolted if, after going to ground, a terrier is put into the earth to persuade the fox to leave. If a fox is bolted it is normally given a good chance to get clear before it is hunted again.

BRACE A brace is two foxes, a leish is three foxes. A pack may catch thirty brace, but it does not catch twenty leish.

BREAK UP The process by which a pack of hounds devours the quarry it has killed. Foxes are almost always killed by having their necks or backs broken, which happens remarkably easily if a hound seizes the fox at these points.

BROW (See Antlers.)

BRUSH The fox's tail is always referred to as a brush.

BUCK A male Fallow deer.

BULLFINCH A fence which has been allowed to grow and which must be jumped through rather than over. (See Jumps.)

CALF A young red deer up to one-year-old.

CAP Money paid to the hunt by a visitor joining it for one day. Most hunts limit people who wish to pay a cap to two or three days per season. A collective noun for the total sum of money collected from the Field on any one day.

CARTED DEER A deer kept specifically to be transported to the hunt country, hunted until it turns at bay, then reloaded into its transport and returned home.

CAST	Hounds can cast themselves or be cast by their huntsman. In either case, the object is to uncover the line of the hunted animal.
CHECK	Hounds check when they lose the scent of their quarry. A check can result in the animal being lost, but is usually just a pause in the hunt.
CHOPPED	A fox is chopped if it is caught before it is on its feet and running; if it is caught by surprise.
CLEAN BOOT	Hunting a man by his own scent, not a false scent, with blood-hounds.
CLEARED	An area is said to be cleared when all the farmers within the area have been seen to make arrangements for the hunt to go over their land.
COUNTRY	A hunt's country is an area of land with known boundaries and which is registered as belonging to a specific hunt by the Association controlling that form of hunting. All hunts must have a properly recognised country, but countries, or parts of them, can be borrowed or loaned. Thus no area should be regularly hunted over by more than one pack of foxhounds. However there is no reason why a hunting country used by foxhounds should not be part of a staghunting, a hare hunting and perhaps even a draghunting country, thus the New Forest contains packs of foxhounds, buckhounds and beagles.
COUPLE	Hounds are always counted in couples, thus 17½ couple is 35 hounds.
COVER	An area of rough ground, moor, woodland, gorse, bog or a farm crop in which hounds may find their quarry.

COVERT	A wood or gorse specifically planted to provide accommodation for foxes or pheasants. Coverts are usually of six to twenty acres.
CRY	(See Tongue.)
CUB	A young fox in the first seven months of its life, i.e. up to the Opening Meet.
CUBHUNTING	Hunting before the Opening Meet. A period when young hounds, young foxes and sometimes young horses and people are taught what to do and expect when hunting.
CUR DOGS	All dogs seen when hunting other than hounds – dogs controlled by the Kennel Club.
DOE	A female Fallow deer and a female hare.
DOG FOX	A male fox.
DOG HOUND	A male hound.
DOG PACK	A pack confined to dog hounds.
DRAFT HOUNDS	Hounds sent from one pack to another, other than for breeding purposes.
DRAG	The stale line of an animal that has moved.
DRAG LINE	A line laid with an artificial scent (i.e. other than an animal or human scent) to be followed by draghounds.
DRAW	A huntsman draws his pack, i.e. selects the hounds he intends to take hunting. He also draws with the pack, i.e. tries to find an animal to hunt.
EARTH	A hole in the ground developed by foxes for their accommodation. They also use drains and badgers' sets.
EARTH STOPPER	The person who blocks the entrance of an earth the night before a hunt, to keep the fox above ground.
EDGED ON	To increase the pace of a pack without breaking their concentration.

ENTERED	A hound is said to be entered when it has learned to hunt its legitimate quarry.
FAWN	A young Fallow deer.
FEATHER	If hounds cross the line of their quarry they will turn up it. They will then follow it slowly, sterns waving, until they are sufficiently sure of the line to speak. This is known as feathering.
FENCER	Few hunts will employ a man solely to mend fences. A fencer will also put in hunt jumps and hunting gates, work in any coverts which come under the hunt's management, and he will help with the earth stopping.
FIELD	The followers of a hunt other than car followers.
FIELD MASTER	The person in charge of the Field.
FIELD MONEY	The money paid by members, subscribers and farmers on each day they hunt. It is over and above the annual subscription and in many countries can be commuted for a fixed sum. Field money in the plural is often referred to as the cap.
FIELD SECRETARY	The person who collects the money due from members of the Field on each day they hunt.
FOIL	Any scent that obliterates that of the quarry.
FORM	(See Seat.)
GATE-SHUTTERS	Two or more people who follow the Field to ensure that all gates are shut, and any damage done is reported to the Master or hunt secretary. With most hunts these people are subscribers who do the job on one day only, either by lot or rotation. (N.B. The fact that a hunt has gate-shutters does not mean that gates may be left

open on the assumption that the gate-shutters are always there to shut them.)

GONE TO GROUND   A fox goes to ground if it enters an earth, drain or set during a hunt and thus brings it to a permanent or temporary conclusion.

HARBOURER   The man who locates the stag that is to be hunted and informs the Master of its whereabouts. Thus a stag that has been harboured is one whose position is known.

HEAD (OR HEADED)   To cause a fox to turn from its natural course.

HIKE (OR HOICK)   Huntsmen use a number of words and phrases when working their hounds such as: hike (hark), forrard (forward), lieu in, rouse him up and cope (come on).

HIND   A female red deer.

HOLD-UP   To hold-up covers means that they are surrounded and every effort is made to prevent foxes leaving. It is a procedure frequently used by packs of hounds during cubhunting, and is also carried out by some packs when there is an urgent need to reduce fox numbers.

Hounds may be held-up, or temporarily stopped. The term is often used when tufters are held-up during staghunting while the rest of the pack is sent for.

HOLLA (OR HOLLOA)   To inform the huntsman, a member of the Field may shout 'gone away' when he has seen a fox leave a cover unless he thinks the hounds are hunting another. He should not do so unless the fox has got well clear. He then puts his horse onto the line the fox has

96

taken, with its head pointing in the direction it has gone. Having holla'd, if he can see the huntsman, he should take his hat off and hold it up in the air. Other hollas: *Tally ho over* may be used when a fox is seen crossing a ride. *Tally ho back* is frequently used during cubhunting when a fox leaves cover, stops and returns to it. *So-ho* is the correct holla for a hare, hence the name of a celebrated part of London, formerly a place for hunting hares. There is also a high penetrating screech which carries, and which may be followed by the above information once contact has been made. Although hollas may be invaluable to a huntsman, if they are persistently repeated they will interrupt his concentration.

HOUND BITCH   A female hound.

HOUND PUPPIES   Hounds remain puppies from when they cease to be whelps until they start their first season's hunting i.e. after the Opening Meet.

HUNT HEAL   Hounds hunt heal if they follow a line in the opposite direction to which their quarry has gone, i.e. in the reverse direction. Unless they are stopped, hounds are more likely to hunt heal on a bad scenting day than on a good scenting day.

HUNTING HORN   A short, metal wind instrument blown by the huntsman. It enables him to inform his followers, and both inform and control his hounds. Generally speaking, the single notes provide information of place and intent; short multiple notes involve a fox on the move and imply urgency and requirement; a quavering rattle signifies the end of a hunt; a long, drawn out two-tone note signifies the end of the day.

HUNT SECRETARY The secretary to the hunt committee. He may also act as Field secretary, and may be the hunt treasurer as well.

HUNTSMAN The man who controls the hounds when they are out hunting.

JACK HARE A male hare.

JOINT MASTER When two or more people share the duties of Master they are known as joint Masters.

JUMPS Obstacles jumped when out hunting may include: cut-and-laid hedge; stake-and-bound hedge; rhine or ditch; bank; post-and-rail fence; wall.

KENNEL CLUB A club which controls the stud books and shows for all recognised breeds of pedigree dogs other than hounds hunting in packs.

KENNEL HUNTSMAN The man in charge of the hounds when they are in the kennels. If the pack has an amateur huntsman, the kennel huntsman is usually the first whipper-in; if they do not, the kennel huntsman is also the huntsman and is referred to as such.

KENNELMAN The man who collects and prepares the food for the hounds and who looks after their lodges.

KNOT (See Antlers.)

LEISH (See Brace.)

LEVERET A young hare.

LIEU IN (See Hike.)

LIFT A huntsman lifts his hounds when he collects them to take them forward on to fresh ground where he believes the quarry has gone in order to save time. Hounds may be lifted to make a cast,

	but they are usually lifted to where the quarry has been seen to go.
MARK	(See Tongue.)
MASK	The head of a fox and the head of a hare.
MASTER	The manager of a hunt.
MASTERS OF FOXHOUNDS ASSOCIATION	The Association of Masters and ex-Masters of Foxhounds. Masters are entitled to put the letters M.F.H. after their name. The committee of the Association is the controlling body of the sport, and its book of rules apply to all hunts which it recognises. Packs which are not recognised cannot be entered in the Foxhound Kennel Stud Book, nor may their hunts hold a point-to-point. Other hunts belong to their appropriate Associations, thus all Masters of harriers and beagles belong to the Masters of Harriers and Beagles Association.
MUTE	(See Tongue.)
NOSE	The scenting power of the hound.
OPENING MEET	The first hunting day after cubhunting has finished. Formerly it always took place in the first week of November, but now it often happens at the end of October. It is a day when everyone turns out looking their best.
PACK	All the hounds belonging to one hunt form its pack. If a huntsman draws a pack, he is selecting the hounds he will hunt on a specific day.
PADS	The feet of hounds, foxes and hares are pads.
POINT	The length of a hunt if measured from A to B in a straight line.
POINT-TO-POINT	A steeplechase meeting for horses that have hunted regularly. It is run by a hunt in aid of its own funds.

PUPPY SHOW	A summer show at which the hunts may display their young hounds prior to the start of cubhunting.
PUSS	Hares are frequently referred to as puss. It is also often assumed that they are female and, therefore, referred to as 'she'.
QUARRY	The hunted.
RAT-CATCHER	The mode of hunting dress worn when cubhunting.
RIDE	A path in a cover.
RODE OFF	Most people will catch a loose horse if they can, however, the first duty of the hunt staff is to care for the hounds, so they may 'ride off', i.e. force to take a different direction, any horse that looks like going through or over the pack.
ROUSE HIM UP	(See Hike.)
SCENT	The scent of an animal is the smell that it leaves when passing over the ground which a hound can follow. Good scent and bad scent are expressions referring not to the quality of the scent, but to the length of time it remains on the ground. Three things affect this: a) the type of surface upon which the scent is laid; b) the weather conditions and atmospheric pressure at the time the scent is laid; c) the animal itself. Certain animals produce a stronger scent than their fellows. Scent remains one of the great imponderables; something that cannot be predicted with absolute certainty.
SCUT	A hare's tail.
SEAT	The seat, or form, is the scrape in the ground where a hare spends much of the day.
SETS	The badger's home.

SETTLE	Once hounds are together, are collectively sure of themselves and, together, increase the pace, they are said to have settled, i.e. settled down to hunt the quarry.
SHOOTS	It is important that country sports and their followers work well together, therefore most Masters try to liaise with shoot managers before the start of the season.
SLOT	The foot of a deer.
SPEAK	(See Tongue.)
SPRING STAG	A two-, three- or four-year-old stag.
SQUAT	A hare is said to squat in its seat or form.
STAG	A male red deer.
STERN	A hound's tail.
STOCK-TIE	A garment worn around the neck when hunting, fastened by a pin, usually (and correctly) a plain gold one. Pins with a fox's head or other ornamentation on them are worn occasionally. The Devon and Somerset Staghounds, which are normally followed by people wearing rat-catcher give a special silver pin in place of a hunt button.
STOP	To fill in the mouth of an earth so that it cannot be used.
SWEAT RUG (ANTI-SWEAT RUG)	A rug made for a horse that has had a great deal of exercise. It works on the principle of a string vest, and should always be used under another rug thus trapping air to evaporate the sweat. The horse is then warm and dry.
SWITCH	(See Antlers.)
TERRIER MAN	The an in charge of the hunt's terriers.
THONG	The flexible part of a hunting whip about 4ft 6in long. The part that, when

hanging down, acts as a signal for hounds to pass.

THREE A-TOP	(See Antlers.)
TONGUE	Hounds do not bark; they give tongue or speak. When all the hounds are speaking, the pack is said to be in full cry. A hound that hunts but fails to speak is said to be mute; a very bad fault. A hound which stands back, faces an animal and barks is said to bay that animal. Speaking and baying do not sound alike. When hounds bay at an earth where a fox has gone to ground they are said to be marking.
TRENCHER-FED	Hounds are trencher-fed if they do not live in hunt kennels but in individual homes.
TRES	(See Antlers.)
TUFTERS	(See Tufting.)
TUFTING	Finding the deer that has been harboured with a few experienced hounds known as tufters, then forcing him to leave the area and any other deer which are with him.
VELVET	The furry substance that surrounds a growing antler.
VENERY	Hunting.
VIXEN	A female fox.
WALKED	Hound puppies of from eight to twelve weeks old go out to farms to be walked, or reared, for the next six to ten months, after which they are returned to the hunt's kennels.
WARRANTABLE STAG	A stag believed to be at least five years old.
WHELPS	Hound puppies from birth to about eight weeks old when they are weaned.
WHIPPER-IN	The assistant, or assistants, to the huntsman.